C000126001

Solace

Poetry of Nature

anthology edited by
{austie m. baird}

Austie M. Baird is a born and raised Oregonian, holding both
History and Education degrees from Eastern Oregon
University. Long before becoming a wife and mother, Baird
connected with the power of the written word, finding
healing properties in both reading and writing. She draws
strength from the beauty that surrounds her and the
overwhelming love of her family.

A.B.Baird Publishing
Oregon, USA

Printed in the United States of America

First Printing, 2020

ISBN: 978-1-949321-14-2

Cover Art Image by Austie M. Baird

{Dedications}

For Gemma –
You are forever my bright star.
{Elowen}

Thank you Zoe,
for reading anything I put in front of you with eager and
helpful eyes. You are a wonderful editor, but an even more
wonderful friend.
{Kate Petrow}

I must thank Austie for including me in this exciting project.
Also to my beautiful family, my loving partner Jonathan and
our baby Boy Loki. Not to forget all my family and friends
who have been very supportive of everything I do.
{Amy Jack}

To those searching for a little light-
when the world gets too heavy,
always remember to take a deep breath
and let the healing in.
{ashley jane}

Thank you to the North Star that caught me in his fire,
and ushered me toward the Way.
{Megan}

To the readers who keep me going.
{Onyx & Amber}

Winds that carry the smell of sunshine bouncing off the
canyons walls & the ones who taught me of your spirit.
{Austie M. Baird}

{Table of Contents}

Kate Petrow
    Bio   p. 1
    Poems   p. 2 - 24

Megan Patiry
    Bio   p. 25
    Poems   p. 26 – 47

Amy Jack
    Bio   p. 48
    Poems   p. 49 – 69

Kait Quinn
    Bio   p. 70
    Poems   p. 71 – 96

Elowen Grey
    Bio   p. 97
    Poems   p. 98 – 115

Ashley Jane
    Bio   p. 116
    Poems   p. 117 – 138

JaYne
    Bio   p. 139
    Poems   p. 140 – 164

Onyx & Amber
    Bio   p. 165
    Poems   p. 166 – 188

Lauren Kaeli Baker
    Bio   p. 189
    Poems   p. 190 – 216

{Kate Petrow}
@littlecloverleaf

Kate Petrow is a student of dietetics and creative writing at Indiana University. Kate is an avid reader and writer because of the beautiful relatability, the innate personal connection, and the escape that can be created through the written word. She is currently working on a novel, and she posts her poetry on Instagram, @littlecloverleaf. Outside of bookishness, she is passionate about nutrition, animal rights, and environmental wellbeing.

Why do you hurry?
        the river says
        through white rushing foam.
Well, I reply
        from the waters edge,
Don't you?
No,
        she whispers,
It took me years
to make the rocks beneath your feet smooth.
It takes me ages
to reach the ocean.
I am in no hurry,
but I also do not wait.
        I flow,
        I bend,
        I move
        s l o w l y.
I lean into the time it takes,
for in that time
there is space to live
        and dance
in dappled patches of the sun's glow.

{slow dance // k.p.}

We walked on pebbles glistening wet,
and the ground beneath our very feet
seemed to tremble
as the trees invited us to dance.

You threw a stone
at the cool, clear stream
and as it skipped along the surface,
I could see our story unfolding,
like ripples do
on still water when disturbed,
reflecting a sky of diamond blue.

{hike // k.p.}

What I saw
was a small pink flower petal—
from a redbud
in bloom, perhaps—
floating on silver water,
swirling toward the storm drain.
And a single crow, cutting
through the air spinning with rain,
his beak stretching
toward the petal,
his bead-like eye set
upon the jewel.
But he pulled up
at the very last moment,
and the petal descended into the shadow
of the drain without pause,
the crow balking and bobbing
his head, his furious mouth opening
to form a shrieking song.
And soaring upward,
a black burr
against the gray.

{a crow in mourning // k.p.}

The marbled sky above Paris
tells a love story—
all wrapped in lavender and gray,
smitten—
and if you listen closely, you can hear it
on the wind.
Deep below the cobbled streets,
it is quiet on the metro,
although the car at the train's end is packed
with people sitting and standing,
clutching the metal poles for balance.
All I can hear is you.
I like the way you talk—
thoughtfully, as if each word
is a wildflower petal.
Your eyes remind me
of the skies back home—
endless blue, reflective
and I never want our stop to come.
But it always did. And now
I just want to return
to when the Paris metro told our story,
all low hum and gentle sway
and one shrill beep
to alert me when the doors would close.
I wish you could remember it the way I do.
I wish I hadn't remembered it wrong.

{unrequited // k.p.}

I'd like to be
forgotten
just as much as I'd like to
forget.
A blurred photograph
on a shelf
just out of reach.
The glass has shattered and
at this point
I only keep slicing open old wounds.
Because   *fuck   you*
and your way of seeping
into the brightness
of what I'm becoming.
I thought I could still see a light glowing
behind the thick window pane,
but it was simply cold, vacant moonlight
settling into the resin—
a lesson.
Once a dreamer,
then I fell,
grounded and learning to love
the scattered pieces.

{fallen, forgetting // k.p.}

I dreamt once
of a deer
white as ash,

and it made me recall a time
that a pale butterfly
landed on me.
She wanted to touch
the skin of my outstretched finger
with her six graceful feet.

For a moment I vanished
into nothingness;
I was made of leaves and sunlight
as she searched for pollen
upon my fingernail.
For a while
she twitched her antennae
contentedly
until she fell from her perch
and floated away
on wings white
as wildflower petals.
And I was left,
wondering, in the evening light,
how something so small
and earthly
could be more important
than I am.

{pale butterfly // k.p.}

My father taught me
not to fear thunderstorms.
We watched them
from the darkened shelter of the garage
as lightning unzipped the sky,
following closely behind thunder quakes.
We counted the moments between them,
our breaths slowing to the rhythm.

One.   Two.   Three.   Four.

I used to ask him how things were made,
and he almost always knew the answer.
Lightning is simply
electric current
built up by frozen raindrops
bumping into one another.

And beside him, I learned:
the sky is always darkest
before the clouds let go
of lifetimes of black rain and jagged
blades of lightning.
There is immense unknowing
contained within
the fattened frenzy of rainfall.
And once all fell still,
the musky scent of rain lingered
long after the clouds parted.

I asked him once
how the earth was made.
And he hesitated before answering,
no one knows.

And even now,
I am unafraid of the storm.
I can sit
in the dark
for a while.

{storm // k.p.}

Have you ever burnt the tip of your tongue
on a memory?

When I really think
about it, all the things I would change,
and all that I'd keep the same
look quite similar.
The distance
between ash
and what we are now
is not so large,
and some days it feels even smaller,
when I am simply water
being shaped into rain or mist
or something more.
I am learning to trust
the hands that mold me,
the clouds that hold me,
as I wait
to fall again upon this earth.

{memory // k.p.}

It is October and things are falling—
golden leaves and acorns
the size of spools of thread
and birds of prey diving
for mice among the bracken.
Rain might fall as well,
tomorrow, or the next day,
racing down fogged over window panes
and collecting in hollow cracks of sidewalk.
The sun is falling too
further toward the blue horizon,
slipping behind the lanky shadows
of red-brick buildings.
And the calendar is falling
closed, pages moving quicker now
that summer's idleness is gone,
replaced by a warmly-lit glow.

Even I am falling—
into the habit of taking deep breaths
and sitting alone
in the silence of crowded rooms.
Falling—
into terms with who I am
today
and who I want to be
tomorrow
and how the space between isn't lacking,
it's growth,
autumn blooming
in what once was empty.

{october // k.p.}

The tiny white dogwood blossoms
looked like gemstones cutting
into the gray tenor
of the wood.
They floated
down from the wet boughs
and came to nestle in the
hollows of my collarbones
with gentle familiarity.

And standing among the bodies
of these trees I thought,
for just a moment,
I became one too— or close enough,
something better somehow—
as my shadow faltered and
disappeared into the dappled shade
of star-shaped leaves.

{something better // k.p.}

I think that who I've always wanted to be
was me all along.
I think the love
I have always ached for
has been mine since the beginning.
There has always been a space
for me here, I just never noticed
the wisdom
of the late October breeze which comes
to rest on weary shoulders.
Mine are learning to relax,
finally— just a little—
within the soothing warmth.
Because I may never be enough
for the expectations of some
but I am here, and I am
not alone.
There are the ones who stayed,
the ones who showed me
that love isn't being enough,
it's being what you are.
Because sometimes flowers are left in shadow,
but that doesn't make the bloom less
than beautiful, less than alive,
their sweet perfume weaving itself
into the rays of this slow-burning sunrise. Reminding me,
just like the breeze;
I am meant to be here.

{here // k.p.}

I want to fall asleep
in fields of wheat
and wake atop the fir trees.
I dreamt once
that I could float on my back
like an otter,
and I watched the clouds form
from the valley stream below.
I wish that I could run
my fingertips over the moss
crawling on each rock,
or create myself
some soft white blossom
to show my gratitude
for the miracles
I cannot explain.
Because I am unsure
how long I can stand here, still,
at the roots of this ash tree
with my face tilted upward,
and I do not know
how long the late summer sunlight
will hold me gently in its looping arms.
But now it is warm here
and now is enough.

{ephemeral // k.p.}

Four seasons ago
I didn't know who I was,
and before that I was a stranger.
And perhaps I'm still not too sure,
but now I have an idea
where I belong at least:
in new and foreign places,
in the fuzzy shadows beneath old trees
where the wind can lift the hair
from my face,
amid familiar blades of grass
that softly tickle bare feet,
and amid rain storms,
walking beneath the pattering of droplets
and letting them soak my skin.

Last year I went out into the world,
and this year, I'll do it again
because to change,
you cannot return home.
And I have discovered
to see the world is incredibly
not enough, for you must
hear it and feel it in your hands, the weight
of what you are.
And to know yourself, you must understand
that all we are is
soil and rain and skin
and perhaps a little something more.
That to be known is simply nature,
like moth to flame,
a cyclic reminder that in time,
the light touches all who seek it.

{new year // k.p.}

The river reflected the world
      in g r e e n ,
and on the still water
I watched two herons
      soar above,
      their toes making ripples
      along the surface
      as they glided.
They disappeared
      and left
      the water rocking and tilting
until it flattened
      into smooth
          green   glass.

{reflection // k.p.}

Late summer evenings always felt endless to me.
They dripped with impatience,
with soundless shadows
flickering upon my curtains,
and dogs crying in the distance.
With the night closing in
and autumnal chill drawing nearer,
I always knew that I was blooming
even in the stillness,
for I felt the growing pains
deep within my chest.
And even now, that pain is smaller,
but still there
and I'm trying not to let this space
inside me ache
with wanting
because I am already whole,
and filled with sunlight.
Even now.

{finding patience // k.p.}

You do not have to apologize.
You are not guilty
for the sorrow that drips
like rain droplets from moss,
nor for the shadows that choke
a sapling of the light.
Feel that beneath the cool breeze,
there is a warmth,
and there is some for you too
if you love what is simple,
if you feel the weight
of what can't be helped
and shed it
in the gentle lapping of clear water.
There is a corner of this rock
already carved out for you,
and the wind will guide you there
if you are patient.

{you do not have to apologize // k.p.}

Tell me,
do you think
you'll have the time
to pause

here? For just a moment,
this moment,
when the sun is caught
on raindrop-speckled leaves.

Because one moment
is all it takes to notice
the snowy owl, who
has been perched

above your head all along.
Her eyes are the color
of frozen lake water,
and her fathers disappear

into the whiteness of snowfall.
I know your day is busy
and you have somewhere
else to be, but trust me

when I say,
this could be important.
This could be what it means
to be alive, and at once

you are already beginning
to understand:
this is what they mean when they say,
life is precious.

{precious // k.p.}

A woman buying birdseed at the supermarket
told me that the feathers of blue jays
are not actually blue.
They appear this way to the human eye
but in fact are brown in color
and the cyan hue is caused by scattering light.

She said this because I'd told her
that blue jays are the prettiest birds,
as if it would make them less beautiful to me.

But what I hope she realizes
is that it isn't how the blue jay looks
that makes it stunning,
but rather the way it moves
from one branch to the next
without contemplating its ability to fly.
It's the way it falls
and bobs in light springtime showers
and the way it turns its head on its side
to regard me with eyes like black gems.
It's the way its thrumming heart
is the same as mine
because the wind speaks to both of us
in the same language.

{birdseed // k.p.}

The flight of owls is silent.

Everything dangerous is, in the night,
like tired tides of feeling
and seeping black inadequacy.
But I am awake   here,
in a grove of my own making,
and I   move
with the intention of understanding
that the knocking force within my chest
is the same as the beating of owls' wings
and the swaying of tree branches
          in a thunderstorm.

I am the ocean and the moon.
I am the wind in the leaves.
I am   w h o l e   already,
in an elemental sense.
And though this silence surrounds me,
I can let it go—
          open palm—
like the clouds do, heavy with rain.

{owls' wings // k.p.}

See your body as it truly is:
a thing of beauty,
a dense forest with canopies of emerald,
with ferns so lush and lichens in vibrant color
spreading soft among the roots of trees,
marigolds and daisies blooming
in fragmented patches of golden sunlight.
How can a forest be judged
for its shape, its size,
when you can stand within its hollows,
shoulder to shoulder with the trees,
holding fistfuls of wet soil in open palms,
letting the leaves tell you secrets of the wind?
You are a vessel of ever-changing life—
an unfurling vine.
And no matter what attempts to desecrate you—
be it a wildfire, or a storm
that threatens to snap your tender limbs, know this:
a forest, even wholly devastated,
regrows with splendor in time.

{your body is a forest // k.p.}

I saw a black bear once,
      in the mountain wood.
His face was the gray-brown color of cedar
bark and he started
up the trail toward us
as if wondering what we were doing
so near his shaded home.
He stared dolefully as we crept backwards,
and then with a heaving
s i g h
he vanished once again
into the bracken.
It was silent,
almost like he'd never been
there at all
and I think,   that is what it's like
             to leave no trace,
             to live so generously.

I hope I vanish like that too.

{vanish // k.p.}

Wildflowers
in sweet autumn air
smell a lot to me
like love.
And I think,
despite everything,
the earth must forgive us.
That warmth you feel
beneath your skin,
that is love too.

{wildflowers // k.p.}

Not even weeds
will grow through the cracks
of this sidewalk.
Forgotten paths, overgrown,
show no footprints.
And when my body is covered
in dirt
and wildflowers grow
on the undisturbed
mound, their perfume clinging
to your palms,
even then
I'll crawl back to you,
because no grave
can hold me down
and no sky,
clear nor gray,
can trap me here.
When my time comes
around, you'll still have me.
These roots and leaves would still
claim me. Long after
my flesh is gone,
remember me.
And when the light winks out
from the painted black line
of horizon,
remember me.

{remember me // k.p.}

We must not forget,
as humans tend to do,
to be thankful for
the way leaves come to rest
on bubbling streams.
And for birdsong.

For the wild way the wind
weaves in and out of branches,
and the delicate manner of cats
as they stretch
in dappled patches of sunlight.
We must not forget to notice
the butterflies' mosaic wings
or the way the sky folds
during a thunderstorm.

Notice too how the mountains
stretch for years above us,
silent, still,
but they do not dance alone,
for the sun peeks from behind them
and calls us back to home.

{we must not forget // k.p.}

{Megan Patiry}
@meganrosepatiry

Megan is an author, Neuro-Linguistic Programming Practitioner, and wellness and travel writer whose work has been featured in the Huffington Post, Kelp Journal, and many more publications. Her avid traveling spirit is distilled into many of her pieces, alongside themes revolving around healing, spirituality, and philosophy, as well as the ancient mystic arts. She writes to cast lantern light on the bridge between science and spirituality, and to begin the delicate blending of art and psychology.

{Solace: Poetry of Nature // Patiry}

Can we return to the mud?
Spread on thick the clay?
Sink into the dirt of the past?
Fall content into the quicksand?

Can we absorb what has soiled our faces?
Can we accept this earthly progress?

... and know
that it is only after
the mess of birth

that we can be brought to the basin -

that we can be brought to the basin
and rinsed clean?

{before the basin // megan patiry}

The gap of you pulls at me
like low tide, running

Water, slick down this heartbeat

The gap of you questions me
in my fullness, still reaching

Is love the feeling of missing?

Or is love the feeling
of complete?

{low tide running // megan patiry}

I'm just a deer in the wood
And — and you're just a hunter

And I've never seen your face
but I — I know the sound

The sound of leaves crunching under

And I know — I know that sound

of a certain insatiable hunger

I know the cold singing
of your weapon
The temporal satisfaction
behind the catching

I'm just another deer in the wood
and there —

there are so many white tails

{white tails // megan patiry}

There is a singing in the distance
I see it between branches
flickering like Christmas

A symphony
of how you never knew trust
so you tested it
(and I offered you my neck)
Of how you never knew freedom
so you ran for it
(and I braided for you, wings)
Of how you never felt home
so you sold it
(and I tucked away the keys)

Of how you never knew love
so you left it

(and I)

And I know the sound of it -
that rebellious pounding of your heart

I know it because I slept there once
and never stopped

You may not believe it
(not many do)
that a love like God could dwell
between a me and a you

and I will not argue
and I will not convince
society has taught you
that everything real
does not exist

But I know that one day
(maybe not too far from now)
the wind will whisper to you
between the trees of time
a story that is not a story
... but instead a truth that will never die

I loved you
raw and real
like the old religion

When we were two kids in a field
before the magic ended

I have not lost sight of the stars
but I realize that
(for many)
reality can make them seem too far

So even as you walk away
Even as our footprints fade

I will whisper to the wind
as a child and a woman and a friend

I have loved you

I have loved you
(and always will)

{the old religion // megan patiry}

Somewhere
Sometime

(Not entirely Here)

The moon rises
and we are sharing a glass
from the same bottle

Somewhere
Some other time

(Not entirely Now)

we've found liquid God,
corked on the shore

Somewhere
On some other sand

(Not entirely beneath our feet)

we share a heart
that can uncork it
easily

Somewhere

The message inside
is not lost in our tides

Sometime

it is consumed together
as one

{Solace: Poetry of Nature // Patiry}

(Somewhere Else)

The lessons were left to Here

But I see
who we are

(when we are not thirsty)

There

{string theory // megan patiry}

Stay in the shallows
I'll swim in the deep

Better the sharks
than the endless wondering

{fathoms // megan patiry}

There are things to be undone
from our blood

Particles of lessons
pumping in fevered replication

Memory transmissions

Sometimes
the filter isn't small enough

and these learnings
- these scratchy-throat teachings -
have created their own cells

Sometimes
we will have to wait

for a higher technology

An evolution in chelation

In extraction

Until then
we must inject the years
and trust

that this is a symbiotic relationship

Until then
Until undone

{until undone // megan patiry}

{Solace: Poetry of Nature // Patiry}

We run to escape the snowfall
pressing urgently upon our heads.

(no, we will ice over)

Forgetting to look down and notice
that it also pushes up at our feet.

The harshness of Winter ... it is not a blanket
whose desire is to cover us in ice.

No.

The Winter urges us to wait
under the evergreen

with a map
and a white-out

until we have been
so shaken and shivered
and defrosted of conditioning
that we finally realize:

being left out in the cold is not a punishment
but a motivation

a pushing under our feet

an urge to take part in seeking

our endless Spring

{spring // megan patiry}

{Solace: Poetry of Nature // Patiry}

The Beginning is a rose

Starting at the outer petals
We sail across ridges anew
Rise like suns over fragranced curves
Dip our eyes in the dew of night rains

'Round we tumble
in hope
toward the center blossom

But often
just when we're certain we've reached the final fold
we slip into a dark cavern

In despair
we claw at the sides

Little do we know
this cave is simply shadowed by Spirit

Little do we know
this is just the darkness that surrounds our seed

The culmination of all our searching

A little longer
A final rain

and we'll arrive

Centered
into sunrise

Into full bloom

{Solace: Poetry of Nature // Patiry}

At last, we are free of thorns

Summer
Eternal

{sub rosa // megan patiry}

Sometimes the sky tires
of its winter clouds
and the same old cold

So tired
that it decides to set itself on fire
lighting up its familiar gray day

.Sometimes the sky finally decides
to prepare for a new temperature

and — and we watch it

We watch it burn in awe

We look up to it
We sing for it
We pray under it

Understand:

There is beauty in changing your season

{changing season // megan patiry}

They will terraform your dirt
into atmosphere

Nitrogen into breath
Magnet into pole

You will plant
starseeds in their soil

Meteor into holy oil

You will whirl and spiral to life

A shimmering beacon
nestled within God's night

And this will be the highest unity

The perfection of duality

And you will not settle
like dust to one another

But rise endlessly
like suns
across the weary past of your eyes

And you will come to know
a Goldilocks zone

where full life
is possible

And you will come to feel home
in an orbit
set to a spin

that won't let go

{goldilocks zone // megan patiry}

I woke today
in the grey dawn of the morning

Took the new steps down
to the Black Sea

The water barely shivered
A slab of onyx universe
cradling my virgin feet

Beams spilled abruptly
over the horizon

Golds refracting into a prism
of everything done

Like light ... escaping a black hole

And I realized then
that it was time

Time to break orbit
To escape heavy gravity

It was time to believe in miracles again.

{even light can escape // megan patiry}

And lover, you despair
when they say nothing is permanent

When they say that things set
just as the sun sets from the sky

But I say,
does the sun not always
- and yet again -
rise?

Does a soul not dwell
in the body, and remain
- even after death -
a permanent delight?

Do not listen to the outer, lover
Tune in to the throbbing heart of it
To the sharp science

Listen to the reality that whispers
nothing is created or destroyed

Listen
to the thrum of forever
that shines at the edges of your memory

If energy is eternity
then we can be that sea

We can be a drop of endless
in this ocean of uncertainty

{that sea // megan patiry}

And then
it comes like rain

When there's nothing left to wash away

Yes

Yes

This is the downpour
that fills you up

{downpour // megan patiry}

There is a home here
in the silent sweat of dewed leaves
and the thick wind through the Baobab trees

A home where alone is fuller
than alone should ever be

The sun rises over the plains to the East
I'll set out for the day

No one to carry but these tools
to till secrets from age-packed clay

I have found this balance

Sunshine
Moonrise
Dusty-eyes

I am clean

This temple
This blood-fueled residence
is my own again
after years
of Colonial footprints

But now ... now there is a familiar knock at the door

and the bones -
the bones shake in the corner

I cannot tell if they're rejoicing
or clamoring in warning

And I wonder

I wonder whether answering
is required
for full living

{knocking // megan patiry}

And sometimes
two rivers merge
the weight of their waters becoming
— not a hindrance —
but a catalyst

to flow faster
across the rock

to slide smoother
along the shore

To descend quicker
over the falls

To arrive sooner

at the ocean
of everything

{dualities // megan patiry}

When your ridges catch fire
consuming the mountains you've climbed

it is sometimes better not to yearn for water.

Instead, if you choose
to push back the rain

to dam the oceans
to invite in the wind
to stir the kindling

and let your world burn

you may notice

that it will be barren and dark
after the consumption

but the soil -
the soil will sing with light

Minerals for a new planet

A new life

You may finally see

that this burning was only Holy Fire

sparked from Heaven
Lit from within

{terraform // megan patiry}

{Solace: Poetry of Nature // Patiry}

And when we look up we can see
into the depths of all we're meant to be.

We are roots
with souls designed to stretch into the sky.

Do not dwell on the dirt.
It is feeding you.

{soil // megan patiry}

I have come to the river
I have come to the rushing river

I have let it take me
I have let it take me under

I have let it take me under and over
and through

And I will not be fished out
And I will not be reeled in

I am a steady ocean
I am the pulsing sea

I have found the Current
This Undertow

Here, I breathe

I have come to Your river
I have finally come to Your river

And I will not be moved

{river divinity // megan patiry}

Hold tight to the sunrise
You're more than midnight

Bury deep your seeds
The roots will set you free

This is the sky
the moon is your growing guide

Now
Finally

the Sun

and you
are the tallest tree

{deeper, higher // megan patiry}

I have slipped off my feet
and stepped onto the winds of a lover

Higher than mind
is where we eternally meet

And when they ask me who you are
and how I always know the weather

I look up
and say,

There is this warm breath
caressing currents across my heart

It speaks:

One-beat, two-beat
Go now, it's lightning-free

It lifts me up from my knees

It carries me to love-soaked shores

It's only request?

That I hold hands
with its breeze

{winds of divinity // megan patiry}

I will give

the way the sky gives the rain

the way the rain gives the growth

the way the growth gives the new day

Even if the flower
cannot sprout
because it's sun has yet to come out

I will not stop falling

Even if this atmosphere breaks
into electric bruises

I will not withhold
that which is my muse

I will paint the ground
and wait

for the love to rise out

{i will // megan patiry}

{Amy Jack Bio}
@embaark

Amy is a creative person, she studied Illustration at university at UCLAN. Always trying in some way to think outside the box. She has dyslexia which has been a hindrance, although it allows her to take words and completely use them in different ways. Amy, who signs her poems A.J., kind of stumbled into the world of writing in 2018 when I suppose to her it was a quick way of expressing her emotions. Even now she doesn't see herself as a poet. Amy hopes to keep sharing and creating whether that be poetry or Art.

Your all in
But I forgot my hand
I mislaid touch
Blue fingers
They shiver their weight in gold
And I lost out to second guesses
To reading between the lines
Con man of hearts
I sliced myself open
Poured every drop of liquid
Until it stopped dry
Pat these dry brittle bones
I'll see you
And raise you
A joker in the pack
Sleight of hand
Lets you cheat your way
To a bluff, with the jack of spades
Shuffle the deck and deal again
As the queen of hearts
Shouts off with his head
His heart follows suit
Blood drips from the wound
So wring him out
Proof is in the pudding

{blue fingers // a.j.}

{Solace: Poetry of Nature // Jack}

Waves they wash your feet
Dipping toes
To feel a shock to the system
Bitter cold makes their way through bones
Sea worn
The seashore sings of merry men
Pirate eyes patched up
Cross like skull and bone
Land mines swim around in vastness
Sailed too far
Weigh up your options
One hand to the other
Overrule kingdom come
Undine goddess of the blue

{waves // a.j.}

Daily dose
Was it one
One tablet to swallow
One look of open doors
Green is green
But did it consume you
Tingle a little
Brushed up on the bones you call freeze reaction
Like it's still
Like it's painted all over your face for others to enjoy
If a colour was picked would it be orange
Warmth rising to blush of cheeks bones
And in the smidge of the pause of breathe
Did you let it sit
Let it simmer
Bubbling up to realisation
Nature is in your palms
Will you lend
Hands

{daily dose // a.j.}

I will chase the windows
Of a sea view
While the wind whispers
Button tight
To hang dry
The elephant ears
Of fly
Fly away
The never forgets are shoulders we like to mooch
The one step two step
The half opened eyes
Pondering the deepest of blue
Waves of sky
Humanity streams
Humanity screams

{elephant ears // a.j.}

I have barked up
The forest of wrong trees
Homegrown planted
Hearing the weavers call
Dress yourself up in refinery
Green as grass
While a perch is picked up on
Taken with hands
Did you know digging is art?
Ground exploring
Dirt to rise
So water sprinkle what we call fertiliser
Sprout of hand
Neck on neck
Measure the stand still
Succumb to crop up

{forest of wrong trees // a.j.}

Did I miss something
Stay grounded
Nose dive
I slice my face open
Hand in hands
Grazing silence
Slicing every part of recognition
Strangers whistle
Deeper
Deeper than the hum of drums
While the world alters nature's view
Gather the flock
The flock of ego
Pictures are taken
Poured like leftovers In goodie boxes for convenience
Did sparing become an afterthought
Misplaced
Borrowed like old books collecting dust
Forgetting to spring clean
Futile like a feather duster
Heavy hands keep sticking their oar in
Like there's no going back
No going back

{gather the flock // a.j.}

Telling tales
Short ones
Long as far as the eye could see
Hill upon hill
Sweetness of autumn
I'd say the colours linger on our faces
Reddish tones burnt In dimpled cheeks
Built in
Its like they are built in
A case of smile you smile reflection
And as palms nestle in two
Season of wide eyed
Knowing lucky is ten
Ten fingers and toes we carry
Wonder of the wanderers
They come in threes

{telling tales // a.j.}

Remember when our faces met fresh air
Blowing my indoor lungs
Where life begins
Our minds are full of what we see is what is real
But is there truth?
Are you caught or freely catching the eyes of substances?
A yo-yo of time stringing the hollow sockets
A plug in of encounters touchable
The nitty gritty of self
Or an opening of display
We carry the listening ear
A pick pocket of the half spoken
To the half speak
Loose of phrase
Tongues sometimes move
But are the words really telling tales of materialised
Woven in and out
Stitched view parcelled in a bow to bow of facts
Or is it your fiction?
Your lies of white
Are you really you or really them
A know it all

{pick pocket of the half spoken // a.j.}

High pitch
I listen in bells
White noise
I call it white noise
No one gets the tones that you speak
The delicate centre
Where I peeled each and every layer
Over and over
Like it was home
Like it was made for me
And you say sum it up
But words couldn't explain it
My body
A heart picking up its pace every time
You say my name
And those quirky habits of yours
Where smiles are simply rooted to never leave
And where you give hands
Hands unfolded so I see the unraveling
Bare-boned
And open isn't a question

{white noise // a.j.}

{Solace: Poetry of Nature // Jack}

I'm going to pack you in
Like all corners
Keepsakes
Where boxes are boxes stamped with dates
There's a time and a place for that
What I mean is
Clean shaven is a myth
Rugged like state of the art romance
Where Back pockets are full of timber
dirty knees & offcuts come in hand
All fours but nobody is running
Nobody is running

{clean shaven is a myth // a.j.}

Did you see it
Hitting the side views of my face
Shade
I am the bobby dazzler pitching to the ink that hasn't quite set
yet
Ridges they call it
I live behind the scenes of the limelight
Where you didn't see it coming is a phrase so loosely on my
tongue
You didn't see me coming
So when dark knights ride daydreams
I will be a helmet hidden face
For I am disguised in a world full of watchful eyes

{shade // a.j.}

Spoilt by greenery
Every patch has been touched
Trace of fingers lined up onto the next one
More always more
Pots of ancestry held with the brush off effect
And Mourning
Mourning is pressed onto my lips
Carrying more than its own weight
Everything aches
Everything silent
I printed my fingers as if they knew the answers
Ink stains
And now it's all gone
Like the look in the eyes of the many grieving
Political bodies agree with the yes man
If only society was a body
A body left in stretch marks
Of the overindulgent stuffing their faces
Lips dehydrated
And the black eyes where everything is not rosy
Wounds that keep opening and the dressing doesn't quite fit
the dressing up
So I ask the question
How did it come to this?

{spoilt by greenery // a.j.}

Bathe in silence
Fill your body thick with tobacco stench
I mean fumes
I mean visibility is limited
Call it a suffering
A case of misplacement
And the bag of bones are limited to season me politely
When stillness catches up
Will you know the difference of outdoors VS in
Every bit
breathing
Every bit
Tasting
Every bit
Smelling
Earth
The Underground of acres
Neglected waistbands you call home
Will that be the death of me
Will it?

{bathe in silence // a.j.}

Hatch
The weeds have tangled their way
Through my eyes of evacuation
Drawing curtains
Droplets of a clear view
Take me back to the see beds
The rush of cold water
Forming over me
Circles of remembrance
A touch of sight
I long for earth
To feel the ripples
The birds echoing
Place of places
Here or there
Fallen leaves
So you see change
Change has hatched on my skin
Birthing new
Shredding
So your eyes
Have final opening
Rise to the occasion
Head at its highest
Day of dawns
Awaken

{hatch // a.j.}

Building blocks
Make a home
Rows and rows as a drive by lists them in your head
Do you paint?
Fill your mind with a thing called fantasy
Make believe I suppose
Family's of 4,3 or 2
A single one
Busybodies not in the sense of eavesdropping
But just living
Living good
Living rough
Living loud so you hear them from the treetops
Or in whispers hoping to be heard
Maybe your one of those or none
I'm sure when you finally sit down at days end
You realise the luck of the draw is by action
Movement get up and go
Go now
Stop the routine and keep building those blocks

{building blocks // a.j.}

Grow old
With hair nets
Woven to fish
Tying tides
A blue sea topples
The watery eyes
Engulfed in you
We take the hits
Together is a home
So our Feet may not touch the ground
But the ride
The bump of humps
Is a roll of laughter
Over the long lines
They call it paths
That join heart of strings
Pocketing remnants of us
Yo-yoing through yours to mine
A spontaneity of the back to forth kind

{they call it paths // a.j.}

Grace us with hands that hold
Woven palms locking on to surface scratching
Nail beds have a story to be told
Dirty rims of inspection
First layer
We slice under thumbs
Dig deep has a way of getting truths
Crossing fixtures
A crease by crease nature
Surround yourself
Inner circles
Round and round they go
Did you look it up?
Garden of weaves
Plucked to be a part of fortune telling tales
Where rock solid is a mobile answer
And Dial tones have a way of ringing ears
Pick up
Pick up palm of readers

{nail beds // a.j.}

Will there be laughing
Crying
A sign of this life
Has little legs that are kicking
So you ride the rivers
The currents
The shade of your eyes
Where we are left guessing
The hop scotch
Of right steps
1, 2, 3 jump
Jump like beans having nothing on you
And the tips of fingers have touched but a fraction of this
world
That's the beauty of it
Peeling
Shedding
Adapting
A layer of you
Blossoming
See you on the other side

{will there be laughing // a.j.}

You pressed on my heart
Revive
They say pinkie promises
To sink
Sink within my bones
So drafts have no cold
And closed doors have someone who stays In the silent hours
We are soundless
Function paused my lips
But you read them
The still framed eyes
Every last drop
And as I stick to your bones
I finally make room In my closed off mind
Taking down the red tape
Let loose
Letting loose lips do the talking
Welcome
Welcome to me

{still framed eyes // a.j.}

Let me tell you a story
About time
I followed it through the alleyways
The dark enclosures
The secluded
Held hands with best of the best
Actors one of two faces
The door tappers where pints of milk were short hellos
And in the line I carried on joining
I didn't realise I was waiting for my own identity
My own free will of legs
That stepped to where I want to be
To go
And speech
I barely left my mark on the talk overs
Fighting in a breed of their own
To strike a pose
Snaps of happiness
But in the true light of it all
I worked out
I see more than they could ever possibly see
A seer of me

{the door tappers // a.j.}

Take the roads
The windy ones
The steps closer
Paddling for gold
For golden ties
Knots
Family of trees
Built in
From palm to dirt
But it's rising
The taste of sweetness
As it trickles the neck
Did you mean for it to run neck deep
Pooling or pouring a wave of sentiments
Sticking to my tongue
As I swill them round
Left to right
Wholeheartedly
Unbuttoned in nature
Silence is less golden
So I speak

{so i speak // a.j.}

Grey earth splashed me
With the trimmings of face reaction
Luke warm
Marigolds hang the marigolds
On nerve endings tip of fingers
Hold it
embody Surroundings
Stand in steadiness
Fragrance of greenery
Circles that go round and round head high
A dressing in regal
In name
A crown of flora
A flowering
Gaia born

{fragrance of greenery // a.j.}

Everything is washed in softness
Draped in silky skin of fluidity
Native Like my tongue is listed in understanding
Mine
Yours
Theirs
I remember roots have a base line
Have a birthplace where everything is watched in the hawks
of man
fingernail deep because that's how I got here
Rose isn't just flower form
It's River deep in chest marks
Trail on trail
Come with me
Come to the wilderness of Mother Earth

{draped in silky skin of fluidity // a.j.}

{Kait Quinn}
@kaitquinnpoetry

Kait Quinn is a law admin by day and a prolific poet by night. She studied creative writing at St. Edward's University in Austin, TX. Her poetry has been published and featured in such places as: VERSES, *Chestnut Review, New Literati,* and *Sorin Oak Review.* She is also the author of the poetry collection A Time for Winter. When she is not writing, Kait spends her time reading, singing, baking banana bread, creating social media content for a local farm animal sanctuary, and binge-watching shows on Netflix. Kait currently lives in Minneapolis with her partner and their regal cat Spart.

August settled in the air
thick as honey—sweet and choking
and nostalgic.
October burst into flame,
and in November,
the leaves danced,
shaking off the gold dust
of summer that settled silvering
on empty tree limbs—like dew drops
on spiderwebs in autumn
—come glistening December,
when any stretch of land
is a graveyard for flowers past;
still, quiet, white—oceanic in every way
but blue, black, and wild
—a fallow field with nothing
to bloom.
And in this voiceless, barren land,
lying somewhere between
the midnight moon garden of paradise
and the infernal blaze of hell,
I am attempting zen.
I am sparking a fire in my gut.
I am planting seeds in my fertile lungs.
I am collecting ice crystals on
the crests of my cheeks and waiting
for the burning,
for the melting,
for the drinking,
for the blossoming.
For my phoenix bones to drag
the ash of their wings from the thawing earth
and r i s e
like daffodils in June.

{the in-between // kait quinn}

Hard to believe these wet acrylic skies, these mosaic trees,
earth's turning, seasons' cycling—
that nature births from science and not spell.
These lush woods of rain-dewed greenery
will soon turn to stained glass
windows of yellow, vermillion, orange, and flame
painting sky nostalgic gold
until they burn and break, their shards cutting
through the air as they return to earth,
leaving branches bare and our bodies vulnerable
to the coming winter's cold.
Their naked limbs will scrape December's ashen sky,
send it tumbling down in cookie-cutter flakes of ice
and bury the ground in a blanket of white, grey,
and mud brown—what's pure one minute
will slip into decay in the next.
And we will survive on sun lamps, baked bread, and quick sips
of air
stolen between whips of wind and ice,
until earth curls back toward the sun,
warming dirt and melting snow,
preparing Mother Earth for her impending births:
new seeds, new leaves, new flowers to grow
into red and blue geraniums
beating like newborn hearts.
And they say there's no such thing as magic.

{seasons change // kait quinn}

Down the deepest tunnel of winter,
I forget what was so inspiring
about the way the sunlight
drapsed through the trees last December.

June, August, amber-dripped autumn—
all had so much more to offer,
to prickle my flesh, to stir my heart
than the drab skin of winter.

Every other season fluctuates
in color, in scent, in the way mercury dances.
Winter drags on, colorless and dreary,
save for the peach sunrises, fluorescent sunsets
that paint the whites and greys
of February a neon bruise
when the sun so chooses to grace us.

I could keep on praising
the necessity of Januaries,
keep writing these winter blues
into moonsilver linings,
but like hollow chests and static skulls,
so does this bleakness get old.

{winter blues // kait quinn}

Of every winter month,
January is the quietest.
The lights flicker off,
the music stops playing,
snow is no longer laughter and magic
but solid and grey as the concrete
buried knee deep beneath it.

Seven-hour-old snow
crunches like a shattered rib cage
beneath my feet,
scarlet brambles sprawl like veins
—like life still flows
in something desolate
—and the trees are bare as bones,
once their meat has decayed and seeped into the dirt
at the bottom of their pungent grave.

Some mornings, I can't feel my nose
or the skin on my cheeks,
like I might be all bone, no blood
to warm the flesh, no flesh
to hold the heat.
Some nights, I can't tell
if I'm numb
or cold
or just dead asleep.

Some winter days,
the space between earth
and sky is a mirror
and I can no longer navigate
up from down,
north from south,
east from west—like drowning
only without a drop of water
seeping into the lungs;
just an ever thickening frost
threatening
to crack me open
and send me shattering.

{january greys // kait quinn}

I have let November settle
on my skin like a sheet of frost.
I have let December blind me,
force me inward, stilled and hushed.

And as for cruel January,
her fingers icicle sharp and gnarled,
I have let her lash and nip and rot what was pure,
and now I stand on the precipice

of the coldest month of the four;
for February will bite and claw and bruise
when I only want to pluck winter out
at the icy roots and dip them,

like my purpled toes, into summer's warm
amber pools of sunlight. I fear
I shall freeze over completely
and permanently before the spring peonies rear;

for there is a certain class of stillness
that takes not again to thawing,
and I don't know how many more days or minutes
I can bear winter's bone-white bareness.

{in both praise & rebuke of winter // kait quinn}

Plunge me root first
into the petrichor-swollen earth,
so my toes may writhe and wriggle
in tune with the earthworms' rhythms.
I want leaves in my hair, dirt under fingernail.
I want to be snow clean and December still.
I want to be the guiding flicker
in ink sea abyss.
I want to be so sewn
to sunbleached, moonlit, river-carved
Mother Earth, that my irises
thaw into lakes; my locks smolder
pomegranate, violet, gold;
that my skin honeys and dews
under amber August sunrise;
and my pupils s w e l l
into wine-spilled galaxies
while my heart swoons
at lustrous call of wolf goddess moon.
I want to be
flame, storm, and earthquake shake
at Mother's magma loin.
At the least, I want
to autumn burn and summer blossom,
fall like first snow, unfurl
like the last peony bloom,
dusty pink under cottonwood-coated June.

{becoming earth // kait quinn}

Februaries were made for you and me—
skin steaming, limbs kindling,
cracks of light through the blinds turning
the floating flecks of us into something holy,
fresh snow and full moon bright as a blue screen,
winter morning spreading amethyst and amber
over the quiet lawns and stripped down streets.
You whisper *I love you* under the glittering dawn,
and I swallow it whole, let it seep into my veins,
down to heartspace, to belly, to settle between my thighs
like a ripe aphrodisiac ready for harvest.
And when dusk settles with its blues and violets
stretching to horizon, shadows creeping across
infinity's lips and melting into stars, I dare you
to peel back the covers—see what the moonlight makes of us.

{aphrodisiac // kait quinn}

Meet me under the autumn tree,
bark black, leaves red, then russet, then ash.
Let us rub our hands gold,
flush our cheeks pink
under the maple, under the oak, under the watchful Aspen
tree.
Come find me beneath the burning,
heat me bronze, paint me crimson,
torch me melted from the inside out,
make forest fire feel like candle flame.
Meet me in October, when I am more wolf than sheep,
more blood than bone—
moon wild, teeth bared.
Untame my copper hair
with wind and leaves, dirt and fist.
Strip me of spring's pollen, summer's freckle,
so that I may know the raw of salt and soil on my skin.
Plant them like seeds in my bones
so that I may know the swell of sea,
the blood rush of letting go.
Meet me under the autumn tree.
Come die a little with me.

{under the autumn tree // kait quinn}

To slip my tongue beneath an ocean,
desalinate its brine in my mouth,
coat my throat with its fury,
echo the call of sirens,
give to the moon's gravitational pull.

To dig my toes into the forest floor,
grow roots from my soles,
sprout wildflowers from my pores,
paint my skin with the changing seasons,
heed the hollow call of the wild.

To reach my hand into the midnight sky,
grab Saturn by the rings
and galaxies by the fistfuls,
lick stardust off my fingers,
dig my nails into the moon's silver glow.

To spend a lifetime with you,
wrap my pupils around your September irises,
my lips around your vermillion heart,
to sink my teeth into your golden flesh,
and carve my name into your ashened bark.

{intention // kait quinn}

When winter locks us behind our walls,
we wrap ourselves in blankets
and take to the southern seas.
Our lips throw sparks
like steel against flint.
Our bellies become warm as suns.
My limbs river through yours.
My body breathes
you in and exhales pearls
until we're all seal smooth skin
and ocean salted.
You quench your thirsty tongue
with my nectar, until I am all
ripened strawberry, hot July, and want.
You slip quick between my thighs,
and at just the right angle,
my blood starts to ripple, roll,
then crest, until I am all crashing wave
and you are the warm shore
I collapse upon.
I drag my body off yours like foam,
carry pieces of you into the day
to lick off my lips till I get that itch
and rush back home,
wet as April, wild as a hurricane.

{my body breathes // kait quinn}

Walking the frosted wood,
fresh drifts of snow take the shape
of my soles, handfuls of leaves
drained to rust still cling to oak,
birch, maple, their bareness sharp
and scraping the sky into ashfall.
Blackbirds fly off their brittle branches
like lines of Poe
flapping dismally in the malefic lack of wind.

Song cracks open the deafening quiet.
A flash of periwinkle, a blur
of azure, a bird with blossomed throat
in winter trills its June songs
under crepuscular spotlight
in the middle of my melancholy winter.

I waft with my smoke breath to his call.
I spin, spin, spin myself dizzy,
pricking my ears to that flicker of warmth,
pupils groping for that ocean bolt
of blue in a colorless wood,
but all I see is an endless mosaic,
of white, grey, and those dozen hues of brown
that swallow all the fresh blood
out of a bruise—my bluebird preacher
nothing more than ghost,
wish, an illumined illusion,
prophetic portent
of the long dark ahead.

{walking the frosted wood // kait quinn}

I come down like rain
in flooding spasms,
seep into you—

your skin
the earth,
your heartbeat,
the wind.

I drip
from tree limbs
shaken thin,

slink along
blades of grass
like caterpillars,
defenseless

against pecking
beaks,
gnashing teeth.

I give you my wings:
use them
for your escape,
discard them

when you're safe.
I don't need them back—
I am in you.

{sacrifice // kait quinn}

{Solace: Poetry of Nature // Quinn}

On the eve of December,
night yawned its endless mouth
around our curves and swallowed us
whole—all heatless and darkness,
barely the promise of moonlight.
But today, the sun has blinked her eye wide open.
In even the deepest parts of the woods,
her hands leak through the branches,
once cursed for being barren, now praised
and draped in golden tinsel.
And the steam hovering over the cold
water's sunrise-stained surface
is something holy;
       so set the church on fire.
The birds come out singing
winter solstice from their thawing throats—
it's all longer days from here.

{solstice // kait quinn}

After a full moon cycle of darkness,
of dirt-capped waves in a sea of endless white,
the sun, for the first time in months,
like sweet tangerine juice dripping across tongue,
has clawed her way through
the trees' skeletal branches and landed
like pursed lips, like orange peels, dipped and stained
in honey and clove, on my frosted over,
cold and contused, blue-marbled statue flesh,
reminding me that Augusts exist and Julys are
wet, thick, and lightning bug lit, and urging
my stilled blood to flow again,
as my blossoming flesh sets to catch
fire, peach, then ripen.

{sunrise // kait quinn}

I'm sorry, little earthworm—milky pink & flailing in the rain,
washed far away from the damp soil you call home
—that I almost stepped on you with my man made rain boots.

I'm sorry for all the friends you've lost under the weight of
us who have invaded the earth, ripped up the dirt, and left
you wriggling & without a home.

It is not the least I can do but all that I can do: carry you—
silky & squirming —in my bare palm
back to the land your ancestors were birthed from
long before mine were conceived.

{earthworm // kait quinn}

That year, spring rushed through the window
on a beam of sunlight,
gathering the dust of winter in her warm, golden palms
and ushering it out the door,
propped open to cleanse the stale air
we'd been recycling since December.

That year, spring melted the snow to rivers,
coaxed the creek farther over its banks
than it had ever gone before,
flooding the walking trails and bike paths,
muddying the fresh sprouts and matted winter grass.

That was the year we'd forgotten to shed
last spring and summer from our shoulders.
That was the year that the sun waited four whole months
to shed a harsh light on the canyons between us.
That was the year that our summers fell out of tune—
one stuck in winter, the other marcescently clinging
to October.

That year, spring came three years too late
to save our hearts from their iceberged cages.

{spring // kait quinn}

I can hear the meadows call,
the sea sprawling toward us,
reaching for human skin to touch,
as if to say: I am here; as if to say: I am you;
as if to say: save me.

Some people's eyes are as wide and wandering as the ocean,
just as heavy, just as deep,
glossed with stars and filled with soul speak.

The roots of trees finger the dead and cry out
from underground.
We decay, and they grow tall.

And the reeds in the meadows sway with my hips.
Butterflies flutter up from the flowers like my fingers
fly up as if to scrape the clouds
out, out, out from gold-laced magenta skies.
My feet sink into the ground and make like roots.
Life whips against my legs and crawls between my toes.
The wind smacks herself across my face, as if to say:
I am here; as if to say: I am you; as if to say:
save me.

And I try to,
I try to,
but I am a mere raindrop
when what you need is a storm.

{earth poem // kait quinn}

Despite all the planting and watering and
opening my heart up toward the sun;
despite how I carry moonbeams in my uterus
and wolf calls in my throat;
despite how deep my roots snake into the dirt,
knowing Mother Earth like
her skin is my skin,
her salt my salt,
her blood the same scarlet as mine;
despite how far I sail away from home
on the backs of bees,
spinning me into wild clover honey;
I will always walk into summer
with a snowflake on my shoulder
and autumn leaves pinned to my back.

{acceptance // kait quinn}

June is a blossoming, a testing of freshly-wringed wings.
July is cottonwood ethereal one minute,
thunderstorm electric the next.
Things get hazy in August,
s
  l
    o
      w
like dripping honey. August is
a lazy crawl to the end of things, the weight of things,
the last gasp of summer air
before Earth begins its next trick: falling apart
to come back together.
August is dewed grass, hydrangeas collapsing,
a respite from rain, a final bloom, monarchs releasing
and spreading their tiger wings to the south,
Willow tree wisdom, an understanding
of endings and youth, cerulean blues that sprawl
into pink and lavender sunsets, nostalgic dusks,
then endless stars
plunging through the surface of Lake Nokomis,
one last trip to the seaside, one last chance for walking
barefoot through the woods, splashing through the creek,
a silent prayer that we've sown and grown and nurtured
something worth reaping.

{august as a poem // kait quinn}

august rolls in on
passing storms, sudden heat wave,
cicadas singing—

echoing summer's drawling days,
sizzling asphalt,
hazy memories.

and fireflies are
stars on earth. bees and flap
of butterfly wings
are her heartbeat.
and August sun drips honey
thick to horizon.

but summer's close is earth's
golden awakening, and I
am ready to fall.

{cicada's singing // kait quinn}

{Solace: Poetry of Nature // Quinn}

soul swings between life
and death; so the leaves fall, so
October burns to

a blue crisp, so ash
clings to seared limbs, so autumn
tilts on golden hinge

{autumn haikus // kait quinn}

There was no peace for me in the neatness
of tied bows and scarlet roses,
dew fresh and tidy
in their full perfect blooms.

I only ever found comfort
in the trees' crimson fading,
the death of things, the cracking open,
ash smoke thick and spilling.

I only found solace in the breaking.

{in the breakdown // kait quinn}

{Solace: Poetry of Nature // Quinn}

Temperature is dropping,
days getting shorter,
clouds keep hiding the sun and spreading
like the sky is a blue-sand shore.
All that's left of summer
are my fading freckles,
are patches of green that have yet to burn,
rosebuds on my shoulders
where sunlight left her flaming kiss.
Soon I'll be more snow than peach.
Soon I'll be more wool than skin.
Soon the whole city will be ablaze in
amber, orange, and crimson,
then wiped clean
like a post-apocalyptic world turned to ash.
We will learn to live on less—
less daylight, less heat, less color, less concrete,
less fresh air, less stability.
Not so soon but inevitably, the sun will return
and melt the gloom, and we will bear
her sting once more, welcome
the kind of precipitation that cleanses,
feel the finger graze of wind on our skin,
kiss the earth with our soles,
and learn how to bloom color once again.

{all that's left // kait quinn}

Yellow me fierce like sunflower,
nostalgic like October maple leaf,
thick as butterscotch, aged as memory,
striking and soft as afternoon slants
of sunlight spinning cottonwood into gold.

{yellow // kait quinn}

In autumn, I am a Phoenix on fire.
In winter, I am constantly trying
to embrace snow, stab of wind that conspires
to still me when I want to rise blazing

before earth's had the chance to suck the meat
off her bones, incubate her next spring birth—
amber thick, bees suckling her pollen teat,
pink peonies blossoming from her dirt

loins. In spring, I will burn in soft florals,
fresh faced and periwinkle eyed, honey
smeared down my thighs, limbs laced in laurels,
rain lush, peach plump. Summer makes me moody.

It took me years to accept ebbs and flows,
settle into the tides, swallow brine,
hurricane rage, siren scream. Now I don't
know who I'd be without mother moon's light

guiding me home, silvering my darkest
nights, swirling my blood into a tempest.

{cycling back // kait quinn}

Two seasons ago,
I was willow tree drooping.
All that weight,
all that pushing and pulling
and dragging across the earth
inflamed me vermillion.
October breathed her chill
over me, landed on my skin
like a whisper:
let.   go.
So I did and I did and I peeled
and scratched and flaked the dead
cells from my flesh;
cried, bled, heaved, sweat
decades of toxins out of my tear ducts,
stomach, pores, and blood stream.

I let November winds scrub me clean,
welcomed
the flurries of frost over my eyelids,
froze my irises over like the creek—
all still surface,
all work underneath. No,
winter is not for hibernating,
not for me.
Winter is for the healing
and stitching and feeling and nourishing
and drinking in the melting
so that I can unearth into spring
a full geranium bloom.

{the frozen creek // kait quinn}

burn. bleed. swell with amber, plum, and vermillion. then let go. let bones grind down to ash. let the snow bury you into the earth. feel the sting of ice. the following numb. turn inward. bring yourself face to face with the inkiest, stickiest, shadow-thick pieces of your soul. peel heart like an orange. taste your own blood. feel it—the pulse there yet. drink, drink, drink in the blizzard. let it swell you to a bulb as the sun returns to melt winter from earth's flesh. claw through the softened dirt, mud coated and sea salt wet. drag pupil up to sun. let your raised fists unfurl into palms. and rise, pulsating and bleeding like a burning sunflower, a softening peony, a blooming scarlet geranium beating to your heart's enduring rhythms. go on. go on. go on.

{how to fall in love with life // kait quinn}

Winter sank her teeth into my skin
until lingering August heat waves evaporated into a distant
memory.
Some days, I can't remember what July sun feels like
on this glaciered skin.
Some days, I feel like I'm just waiting
for sun to hit horizon and bloat the atmosphere with
moonlight
just to get one day closer to paradise—
honey sticky, steam bath hot
—or whatever comes
when the blood stops.
And this battle of longing and want always ends
with pupil up against stars,
and I remember where I am,
that I stand on a spinning orb and every season,
every day, every moment is ephemeral.
And suddenly, winter is no longer a waiting
but a gathering, a curling inward,
an inky midnight sky without which
nothing aglow could shine.

{the welcoming // kait quinn}

{Elowen Grey}
@elowengreypoetry

Elowen is a poet and self-proclaimed "creature of the wind". She loves exploring the themes of light and dark within the human experience and tries to capture these moments with as much honesty and insight as possible. When she is not writing, she can most likely be found in a cozy bookshop or out exploring the natural wonders around her.

you are the storm
that separates
branches from tree
you are the storm
that uproots me

{uprooted // elowen grey}

i wait for the sun
to come out today
for i need to be held
in a way that is not
composed of hands

{held // elowen grey}

when i say
that i did not expect this
what i mean is:

that i wonder if nature knew
if she already imagined
her flesh scarred
by flames

the scent of spark
ripping through limbs
a wild consumption
transforming a landscape

green and brown

    going

       to
           black

contingency plan:

that is to say
the fallen tree becomes the ground
that will grow the next generation

the earth welcomes back her own

and I...

i wonder if the soil will take me back too

{you will find me in the ashes // elowen grey}

i loose my senses
to the wind
and let it carry me
crisp
cold
up into the branches
of a tree
only to
let me go again
to the
scent of sunday
a soft decay
as one season
gives way
to the next
until unmeasured
time and breath
are all that are left

{the scent of sunday // elowen grey}

i do not control the current
all i can do is surrender
to the waves

{flow // elowen grey}

{Solace: Poetry of Nature // Grey}

i uncurl my hands
in the warmth of the sun
hoping my heart
can learn to do
the same

{a handful of sun // elowen grey}

i don't feel
like rising today
maybe this has
all been chiron's doing
this pulling the sea up
from the bottom
and draining
it all away
he asks me to look
at every broken bone
and shattered piece
that i have long since
hidden from sight
he asks me to hold them
to honor them
to lay them to rest
in the fertile soil
that i have cultivated
in my heart

{the wounded healer // elowen grey}

{Solace: Poetry of Nature // Grey}

i am waiting
for this wind
to breathe through me
like a garden
gently disturbed
ready to
bloom

{the waiting // elowen grey}

nature herself
has littered
the earth
in golden and
fiery hues
a blazing testament
to the power
of surrender
and the beauty
of october days
caught in the
undressing winds
of change

{winds of change // elowen grey}

break up
this fallow
ground

      turn the earth

the landscape
of what once was
can no longer support
the growth

      of living

expose tangled roots
remind them to breathe

let it all go back to seed

{a necessary part of growth // elowen grey}

this day
says hold me
like glass
like breaking
like all the ways
i already
know to let go
and falling
has become
a second nature
of rising
and all the colors
of a sunset
are a hello
and good morning
a moonlit greeting
for my darkness
an embrace
of silence
of truth
of naked heart
of me

{the second nature of rising // elowen grey}

november
takes me apart

bit   by   bit

marigold
peach
scarlet

nature already knows
the steps to
this dance

the creation
of space
the hollowing out
and stripping down
to the essentials

and i ask
this unveiling life
to tuck me close
to tuck me in

to let me blossom
in this sinkhole
of disassembled
circumstances and
shifting patterns

let me be
humbly be

        mine

in the midst
of this storm

{november // elowen grey}

the rain falls here
and the mist
clings to my clothes

     soaks me to the bone

and I feel the need to stay
to freeze myself in place

to hold this holy moment
for all that it is
a cleansing
redemption
rebirth

i have let pieces of myself go

     here on this rock

i have become more like the moss

i found myself in a hard place
and I have learned to grow

{i am the moss // elowen grey}

clouds
pass through sky

        pass through me

like hope to contain is futile
there is no box
strong enough to hold

        freedom

and the wind knows

she leads with unseen hands
to the edge of me

        and i let go

unsure if this is flying or falling
for once i do not care or fear
only feel

the power of surrender
and the life that flows through me

i stand at the edge of wondering
and in this moment

i am the wind

{i am the wind // elowen grey}

maybe not all of me
is trembling cloud
ready to pour
but at the heart
i ache
with a full
that i cannot control
and i feel the running
and slipping through my hands
like time
and hope
and maybe not yet
this territory is uncharted
and the landscape
of my heart an unknown
would it be dishonest of me
to claim this as familiar home?

{nimbus // elowen grey}

there is a sacred light to winter
though we feel the darkness most

there are lessons tucked
in the rhythms of life
treasures to be found
past the stripping of branches

the cold
the barren

when the view out my window
looks a lot like my heart

i pull up a chair
observe
find the beauty in this too

spring will come
the trees know

they do not fret
they trust they have not
met their end

{sacred light // elowen grey}

time slows in the woods
like the pages of my life
steady and still

i feel no need to rush
the next chapter

i only want to hold each second
with simple devotion
breathe each breath
with wonder

take in the sounds of the river
like song
like lullaby
like a mother
welcoming me back

like roots holding me
through this storm

{the place that steadies me // elowen grey}

the earth holds seeds
just like my heart

do not let the
frozen over landscape
fool you

there is life here
resting
gathering strength
testing roots
far below the surface

and i am here
to humbly trust

in the visible
and invisible growth

because the sun goes down
and rises again
i feel it in my bones

even now
as i face this wind
there is life hidden here

do not forget
there is life
and fruit
on the other side
of this season

{the other side // elowen grey}

i watch the light
bend and slip
over the rigid horizon
and i feel at home
in time
in the gentle
movement of the sky
how the sun continues
to shine
when the mountains
do not move
and how good things
grow in the valleys of life

{valleys // elowen grey}

somehow
you hold the shore of me
while i am all waves
and crashing

you settle the wind
the pull of the earth
and i am a witness
to this grace

{you still the wave // elowen grey}

i wonder
if you caught
the sunrise today
if we both sat
in humble
adoration
as silent
witnesses
of the same
moment

i wonder
if your spirit
warmed
at the sight
of nature's
palette
if closing
your eyes
meant a different
way to
memorialize time
and i wonder
if you wonder
about me
too

{meet me in the memory // elowen grey}

time opens a flower
like the body heals a wound
nature has a sacred course
and I learn to walk it well

{in humble wonder // elowen grey}

willows bend
to speak
my name

and i am lost
under her
branches again

as if all
that matters
in the world
is right
here

{wind + willows // elowen grey}

i find myself
in the abandoned places

the places where
ruins rewild
and nature mends
all that has fallen

i let these dry bones
sink into the uncultivated
like rain
like breath
like maybe this is not the end

beginnings come on the
backs of letting go
and I hold the fallow
unlived space within my chest
and welcome it home

{my ruins // elowen grey}

{Ashley Jane}
@breathwords

Ashley Jane is an indie author and book editor. She previously worked as a substance abuse counselor and still consults as needed. Ashley has been writing poetry off and on since middle school, but she has only been sharing her words online for a few years. You can find her on most platforms at @breathwords. She loves music concerts, traveling and true crime dramas. She currently lives in Alabama with her husband and their one child, a rescue cat named Shadow Monkey.

morning comes,
tendrils of light
untying
the tethers
of another hard night

we barely sleep,
and we never dream,
too consumed
with maybes
and what ifs
and so many whys

our hearts were once
a place of wonder

but they've become
barren fields,
a wasteland of sorrow
in a world
once called love

{long days, hard nights // ashley jane}

you tell me
that you can feel summer coming
but my veins
are still spilling winter
my throat is frozen
in syllables
that no warmth can thaw
and these lips,
well,
they are no closer to spring
than they were
the last time it snowed
i wish i knew the secret
to unleashing the sunshine
you keep telling me
lives in my bones
but i'm afraid my shadows
have always been
e x p e r t s
at keeping things hidden

{only winter lives here // ashley jane}

vines of gray
stand out from the wintergreen,
creeping twilight with a grasping hold
on the last bit of life still growing within us,
a mix of magic and desire and shadows that waver
we perch on the edge of dreams,
coaxing covered secrets
from the den of mother nature herself,
searching for a way to stave off the inevitable ending
we lie inside a tomb of spring's dying blooms
we steal a stone from the hollow
where winter rests her head
she offers crystals of opal and emerald,
whispers from within the earth
where she makes her home
we are too often summer drenched in darkness,
autumn clinging to our bones,
waiting on the change,
the end of something,
the death that follows us,
the raven speaking in the language of nevermore
—

let us shake off the dust of this despair
i am too restless to keep standing
in the land of rust and ruin,
too tired to keep wandering in places
that have never seen true light

{let's paint the skies in shades of divine // ashley jane}

winter's breath has left
its unwelcome mark,
frosted glass
hiding the light of a new dawn
we open the windows
and bathe in the sunlight
as it paints the skies
in garnet and gamboge
we watch the snow-kissed flowers bloom
and it reminds us
...so will we

{these vines of ours aren't withered yet // ashley jane}

the clouds part,
and sunlight spills
through open windows,
like fingertips reaching out,
like strands of magic
playing piano,
a sonata
against cool skin
like the kind of warmth
that tempts us
to
rise
up,
like happiness
like harmony
like hope

{sunlight symphonies // ashley jane}

{Solace: Poetry of Nature // Jane}

hazy days painted
in all shades of bittersweet,
and we
long for light

for those bright rays
to wake the sky

we watch sweet daybreak
push the dark away

we yield to the warmth
we rise with the sun

{today will be a good day // ashley jane}

the slow sweep
of a sunlight shimmer

daylight breaking free of its cage,
wisps of yellow floating
between petals
it dips behind the noise

softly, softly
it floats between the apple blossoms,
tendrils of topaz
coiling around our gentle hearts

we breathe
we coalesce

{this is how we heal // ashley jane}

i have seen the wind,
watched it move
through the trees,
listened to its howls hushed
right before the storm

i have felt its strength
as it tore through towns,
and i have felt its gentle touch
on soft nights
after the rain stops

if i listen closely,
i can hear it speak
it tells me
to let it out,
all the things i let build within

it tells me that the wildness is free
and
so
am
i

{freedom calls // ashley jane}

we breathe in waves
of courage
of strength
while treasonous clouds
rain anxious doubt

the pulse of nightfall beats
a chaotic melody,
but the misty moonlight
brings threads of peace

we wake alone,
anchored to the earth
all of our dandelion worries
take flight with the wind
and we flow with the flowers,
curiosity alive in our veins

{the grounding // ashley jane}

the windows are open
the cold air is winding through,
taking with it the last days of autumn
and ushering in the arrival
of the first snow

blackbird is playing on the radio,
the foo fighters's version
i was never a fan of the way
the beatles sounded,
but the lyrics are good

the night is all lush darkness,
and i am watching crystalline flakes
decorate deep sapphire skies,
procrastinating sleep again,
too many haunting dreams
and the dream catcher above my bed
hasn't worked in ages

but i suppose
there are far worse ways to waste time
than entranced
by nature's midnight magic

{nature brings peace to my style of restlessness //
 ashley jane}

there is something in
this december air
whispered pleas
telling you — now
now is here
fold your cares into paper lanterns
and set them free
lay your anger upon the fallen snow
let the cold steal its fire
let the wind steal the ashes
let those feelings go
that kind of fire
will never keep you warm
watch the embers become
something new
something better
a string of soft silver sighs
blooms of bronze brilliance
written in the stars
like shining christmas lights
like ice-kissed crystals
like a shimmer of ink and shadows
spilling across dark pages
breathe
it
in
and
e x h a l e

{light your lantern and listen to the earth //
ashley jane}

{Solace: Poetry of Nature // Jane}

sunlight beckons,
wisps of lemonade light
across blush skies
i place typewritten letters
in old glass bottles
they sail on silken waves,
little sips for those whose hearts
require escape from the winter dreary

{come closer - let these words warm your bones //
  ashley jane}

sunburst
and untamed waves,
restlessly basking
in the shining rays

our wild hearts unbroken
our souls entrusted to the ocean

this is the perfect refuge
for wayfarers,
our troubles drowned
in the healing powers
of runaway waters
and the daring deep

love found
in the chaotic currents
of a stunning sea

{thalassophile // ashley jane}

it is still spring
we are drenched in sunlight,
taking pictures
beneath the cherry blossoms
i watch the petals tumble to the ground,
and it is the most beautiful death
i have ever seen

you see,
the cherry blossoms do not wait for autumn
before they fall apart
they bloom and fade
without regard to seasons
or expectations
and yet,
no one minds that they do not shine
as long as the tulips
or the plum trees

the world still moves on,
admiring the dogwoods and then the pines
and i wait
patiently
until the cherry blossoms bloom
again

{some things are worth the wait // ashley jane}

{Solace: Poetry of Nature // Jane}

my veins are exhaling poetry again,
words rolling through me like waves,

a fickle tide of trembling prose
soaking the pages of lost sea scrolls
until the words wash up on distant shores,

an aging notebook filled with ghosts,
verses read by other lonely, aching souls

{did you find yourself in these lines? // ashley jane}

you shake the branches
of the nearby apple tree
and fruit tumbles to the ground

you stand in awe
that nature bares her wisdom

like the light
of the sunshimmer
and the glow
of the starburst

in the softest hum
of butterfly wings

i bloom like a seedling
i float along the moonbow
i transform like the caterpillar

and you stand in awe

{awe // ashley jane}

i always wanted
to be one with the moon,
but you told me
i was wasting my time on fairytales,
silly things that don't really exist

so i traded wishes for facts
and *tried* to never look back

much to your disappointment,
i was never very good at forgetting

these days
i revel in majestic spells cast by citrine skies
i enjoy the deep blue oceans
and let the waves wash my worries away
i listen to wild whispers dancing on the wind,
carrying messages from distant lands
i live in the balance between day and night,
finding magic in moments that others never notice
and the moon,
well,
it knows all my secrets
and it taught me that nature
is the most beautiful
fairytale of all

{give me fairytale over the bleak of your reality//
ashley jane}

{Solace: Poetry of Nature // Jane}

we fly south,
a blend of chaos and oxygen airborne
above an ocean wild with waves
we crash into the shores of a new wonderland
and float west inside a sea of stolen warmth,
we are swept up by a whirlpool
with no lighthouse to guide us,
watching with uncertain breaths
as daybreak thaws the pitch-black skies
and the sun pushes away the foggy haze
leaving the walls to break,
the ice to shatter,
this powerful magic to race into our veins
and we
become the warriors,
our poetry echoed across vacant spaces
we tiptoe north,
walking within the rising water garden
filled with paper stars,
we search for the ruby lotus
and sip on its wisdom
in silence
until our hearts beat in sync with the tide of time
that rushes around us,
through us
we move east against the current
and let the froth and foam
rinse our souls clean

{meet me at the place where we wash up on shore //
ashley jane}

{Solace: Poetry of Nature // Jane}

lavender heavens and turquoise tides,
a perfect melding of land and sky,
and we live within the evergreen trees,
listening to the wind's soothing reverie,
our hearts seeking clarity
from the sun and stars
while our souls reach out for something holy

{dance with me in the clouds // ashley jane}

i whispered my oath
as cobalt waves
crashed against the shore
i made my promise,
bound by wind and water,
tied to land and sea

and there is no vow stronger
than one held
by the ocean's depth

{forever and always// ashley jane}

wild is the wind that listens
as we sing songs of the deep,
notes of melancholy
placed in the arms of blue sea waves

we count our blessings
as afternoon gives way to evening,
the harvest moon painting the sky
in shades of russet and gingerline
while we are draped in colors
of gratitude and forgiveness,
our heavy hearts a little lighter
since the currents lifted
the weight of our worries,
the nights a little warmer
now that our seasoned souls
are blanketed in something
that feels more like love

we settle into the serenity,
let it carry us into morning
where the sunrise greets us
we become rays of light
we become the softest shine

{we are harbingers of hope floating on the breeze//
ashley jane}

the sky is a jeweled canvas,
flecks of magic within a sea of black
i feel the cool touch of autumn
making its home in my abandoned bones,
and i can breathe once more

{some souls were made for the fall // ashley jane}

dusk to dawn,
midnight fog
fading into morning dew,
sunrise and vermillion skies

and i
am captivated
by the way
flowers bloom

inflorescence,
each petal unfolding
as honeyed harmonies
float
on the wind

{i wake with the flowers // ashley jane}

earth hovers
in a galaxy of goddesses
saturn dresses in iris rings
neptune is wrapped in waves
of amber and amethyst
venus descends,
february stars shimmering
like pearls in her hair
and we are
e n c h a n t e d,
two hearts in the snow
we revel
in the beautiful cold,
in the light of a full moon,
in showers of pure magic
the world is falling together
mercifully
and so are we

{cosmogyral// ashley jane}

walk with me
i want to take you
somewhere far away
i want to show you how to move with the waves
do you see it now?
the way the ocean
always rushes back to the shore?
it races and rages but it always returns
can you taste the sunlight on your tongue?
it is fresh berry and honey dew
it is sea salt spray and coconut
it is sun-kissed skin
and miles of horizon
and i am a part of it
do you feel it?
you are a part of it too

{it is within us // ashley jane}

after death,
we become part of nature's decadence
we soak into the soil
and rise alongside the tree roots
we are buried in the dirt
so that we may grow with the garden mums
we let the sunlight dance
across our petals of promise
because we hope to blossom into something new

{we are a new breed of blooms // ashley jane}

we are a force of nature,
the rise and fall of a storm
that doesn't know where to land

some days,
we are impossible to understand,
emotion carried on howling winds,
hearts that race
like wolves
running through the trees,
and i am not always sure
if we will make it
through the forest maze

but some days,
we are the zephyr,
all soft breeze
and gentle touch
and sunlight after the rain,
souls basking in the warmth
beneath clouds
that no longer know
the color gray

{force of nature // ashley jane}

winter is an exquisite art –

i. the morning land is dressed in clear lights and a blanket of
sparkling snow pearl white

ii. silent nights bring dark peace,
pockets of hidden shadow spaces
nestled in a moonlit forest

iii. my soul flows through the back yard
inside buried tunnels of ice
on a spiritual race to reach the silky river
that flows wild within the veins beneath my skin

iv. this majestic wonderland whispers my name,
stirs my soul, and settles into my bones

v. i am breathless, speechless,
e n c h a n t e d
by the effortless way
nature weaves tales of magic

{let me tell you about my favorite season //
  ashley jane}

{jaYne}
@_a.jayne_

jaYne grew up in the Pacific Northwest and, consequently, enjoys most outdoor activities, especially hiking and biking. Most of her poems are written while she is out enjoying nature. She feels there is no better way to communicate her thoughts and feelings than through natural imagery. Besides being outdoors, jaYne also enjoys drinking Pacific Northwest wines and craft beers and reading Romantic Era literature, which mirrors her strong appreciation for nature.

The sun rises in the east.
A rabbit sits
facing west,
watching its growing shadow.
It scampers in fear
of the darkness
it has created.

{frightened rabbit // jayne}

The black bird—
always calling out,
infinitely lonely.
Sun.
Rain.
Snow.
Alone.
Even with its murder,
always calling out,
infinitely lonely.

You think it is
such an ugly sound.
I think it is
quite comforting.
I hear it,
late at night,
in the beating
of my heart.

Infinitely lonely—
yes.
Comforting—
yes.
I am not alone
in my loneliness.

{black bird calling // jayne}

There is a field
that I've been walking by
for the past fifteen years.

When I was ten,
I'd stop to click my tongue,
hoping the cows
would see I was
one of them,
come to me,
and let me speak to them
with my hands.

When I was fifteen,
I'd stop to take photos
of the contrast
of red bellied robins
chirping atop the barbed wire fence,
blue skies reflected
in the puddles below.

At twenty-five,
I see garbage,
rot,
decay.
The cows are looking starved
of music now
that the robin no longer
stops here to sing.
And the puddles are too muddy
to reflect anything.

It's the same field
that filled me
with awe
and wonder for life
in my youth,
but now all I can see
is the havoc
man has wreaked
on a world that meant him
no harm.

{everything is more beautiful in the eyes of a child //
jayne}

The moon
and stars
and the cat's eye
and Andromeda—
they were never
the final frontier.
It has always been death,

the only place from which
no one has ever returned
with a clearly figured map.
We only know there is a river
whose flowing transcends time,
whose crossing is paid for
by the ones left
on the distant shore
as the traveler waves goodbye.

{styx // jayne}

I live encased in glass and cement,
a box of anger and noise.
This is the world.
This is human nature.
It has drilled its way into my brain
like a hungry maggot.
I have lost myself in it.

The disconnect is so deep
that when I find myself out in the wild,
its beauty seems unnatural.
How can waterfalls and skyscrapers
exist on the same Earth?
No, the trees must have come from Heaven.
It would explain why
they are always reaching for it.

{parasitic existence // jayne}

I used to pluck them up
from their homes
and watch them crawl
across my palm.
I'd run my finger
down their backs
and wondered why
they curled up so tightly.
I was no threat.

It's 20 years later, and
I don't hold them anymore.
I don't wonder.
I find myself
curled up in the palm of Love,
waiting for it
to let me down,
begging it
to do so gently.

It's strange how,
as we get older,
we become afraid of
more things.
We become afraid of
what means us no harm.

{armadillidiidae // jayne}

The sun filters through the curtains,
across the room,
and into my eyes.
It's January,
but it feels like spring has come already.
The birds twitter,
and the dogs bark,
and the clouds flutter lazily
like butterflies.

But the breeze has its bite,
and though I'm inside,
I can feel the gooseflesh
raising on my arm.
So sweet,
so sweet a sight it is.
The flowers are all poised
for blooming,
but

I am the poppy
that never opens.

{a glimpse of frozen spring // jayne}

Three Things Church Taught Me:

    1.   My soul is a golem. I sludge
through this life leaving
everything I touch in darkness.
It does not matter the image I
was crafted in. I cannot touch
a flower without plucking it,
cannot pluck a flower without
sadness for its passing from
perfect into slow rot.

    2.   Other people can't save you.
Most can't even love you. They
will give you a cup full of rain
and tell you that it's holy water.
And they believe it. Then they
turn their eyes to Heaven to ask,
"Did you see that? Did you see
how good I am?" And they will
turn their backs on you in your
most wretched state, thinking
they have made you clean or
not really caring anyway.

    3.   God doesn't go to church. He
is out in the world, calling to
those brave enough to seek
Him out. He is in the field of
flowers so vast, I could never
ruin all of their softness.

{three things church taught me // jayne}

The moon is calling,
and I must go
to the end of the earth
where its glow is brightest.
I must escape
the chatter of
the morning birds
who know nothing
about which they speak.
The leaves fall
most swiftly
in the night,
erasing the footprints
of past mistakes,
ensuring they cannot
follow me.

The moon is calling,
and I must go
to the end of the earth
where I can peek
just over the edge—
where I can bend down,
cup my hands,
and drink
from the pool of stars.
The sun never offered
such stillness.
The light never healed
my lonely heart.
It only ever hid it.

The moon is calling,
and I must go
to the end of the earth
where it is all lignin
and vanillin
and angels' trumpets
and softness.
The gods of day
crumble and lay silent
with no one to worship
their stony souls.
The universe makes them
nothing.

The moon is calling,
and I must go
to the end of the earth
where I can exist
as I was made to be.
Become with me.

{transcendental soul // jayne}

Your anger
is too heavy to carry.
Set it down
in the river.
Let the water pass
over it.
Let time pass
over it
and make it small—
so small
you cannot find it
to pick it up again.

{continue // jayne}

Somewhere out there,
in distant fields
undefiled,
the rain collects in pools
so perfect,
they reflect the crystal sky.
Water is born from Earth,
and to the earth,
it must always return.
Sinking.
Seeping
back into darkness.
The sun laughs lightly
at the toils of that which lies below,
that which strove to be more
than it truly is.

{a natural order // jayne}

Trees lay scattered
like sun bleached
broken bones.
All their flesh
has been eaten away,
has become earth
once more.
And I wonder about
the harsh and cruel forces
that felled such life.
But then I see
the rainbow of flowers
that grow at their sides.

{seeing in circles // jayne}

Life is a mountain
we all climb.
It is all uphill.
Roots grow from nowhere,
twist about our ankles,
bring us to our knees.
We bleed and bleed and bleed.

But the earth smells sweet
like the sunlight
that pours through
the ever thinning trees.
On our knees,
we are perfectly poised
to look up into it.

So we continue climbing,
hoping to reach it,
hoping to hold it in our palms.
But no mountain touches the sky.
No hands were made
to cradle the sun.

We are all really chasing
waterfalls.
We cannot see
what lies beyond the veil.
We reach our fingers through
to emptiness.
We venture to the other side,
into cold and darkness.

But somehow,
the light permeates
through the curtain,
and there are places
it reflects off all the droplets.
It glimmers like the stars
we spent our nights mapping.

And so even in this place,
we know that we belong.
We know that we can close our eyes
and finally have a rest.

{the view from the other side // jayne}

His eyelashes fan out
like the sun's rays—
the kind that push through storm clouds
to illuminate the tops of trees
and coax my thrush of a heart
out of the bramble.

His eyelashes fan out
like the sun's rays—
the kind that open the morning sky
like golden wildflower petals
and invite my hummingbird heart
to drink of a life so sweet.

His eyelashes fan out
like the sun's rays—
the kind that are depicted
in stained glass murals,
the kind that still my fluttering heart
in silent worship.

{and his eyes are the sun // jayne}

Come into the dream with me
where we lay our bodies down
on soft clover beds
and hum lullabies with the bumblebees.

Come into the dream with me
where the birds sing,
where the butterflies flutter and land
on our outstretched fingers,
where nothing beautiful fears
the work of our hands.

Come into the dream with me
that does not require sleep,
that lets us feel
with our eyes wide open,
that lets us see.

Come into the dream with me
and never let the world outside
our cloud castle haven
uproot us from the sweet soil
where we have determined to bloom
together.

{come // jayne}

I hike through fields of wildflowers
whose names I do not know.
I used to marvel at their existence
and take it as a sign
that there is a benevolent god.
I used to let their beauty
wash over me like sunlight and oxygen.
When the periwinkle butterflies
or softly purring bumblebees
found peace on their petals,
I did too.

But now my mind is racing
to catch up with my heart,
to put words to how I feel.
The shadows bend under the wooded ridge,
and the white flowers glow like candles.
Red flowers scatter across the meadow
like flames are licking their stems.
I can almost hear the ring of the bluebells
in the lazy mountain breeze.

And there is a flower
that looks like lace,
that looks like it should be held
in a glass jar on the windowsill above the kitchen sink
as bubbles rise and you sing
and I turn the music down
to better hear your voice.

And I wonder at the names
of all these wildflowers.
I spend hours trying to figure out
how best to describe them,
how to paint a picture
with their exact pigments and lines,
so that your soul can vibrate
at the same frequency as my own
even though you are not here
to see them with me.

{sundays are for worship // jayne}

{Solace: Poetry of Nature // jaYne}

Just because there are thunder clouds
looming overhead
does not mean the sun has disappeared.
It is shining ever so strongly
on the other side of the dark,
working diligently to dissipate
what seems to weigh so heavy.
There is always rain
preceding a storm's breaking,
but soon the light will come through.
You know this about the sun.
I know this about you.

{brighter days ahead // jayne}

Indistinguishable—
you and I.
Yet
I am lilac,
and you are
butterfly bush.
I may be
sweet,
but beauty
and softness
are drawn to you.

{the difference between us // jayne}

You sing like daydreams,
like birds
and petals
and the glittering
of snowcapped mountains.
You know the stars
in every galaxy
by their name,
and you hold them
in your hands
like lanterns,
casting everything in
a beautiful glow.
Your words
drip from your mouth like honey,
and the lost would traverse through deserts
just to taste you.
But you are mine.

{pride // jayne}

I learned about creation
in a time lapse video
of a red red rose
blooming at rapid speeds.
The petals opened
to drops of dew
forming and shimmering
in the light.
Cut scene to stars
swirling,
in Van Gogh fashion,
around a waxing moon,
to the sun rising
and falling
and burning up the sky,
making gold
of the tall and bending grasses,
to the wolf howling
into nothingness,
to a returning howl in the distance,
to finding home.
I learned about creation
in a way that made me feel
like I was devoid of life,
like I did not belong.
But when you said
you love me,
I felt that red red rose
blooming,
its petals stretching
between my ribs.

I fell under the dizzy spell
of the stars
and the moon
and the sun.
I have found
home
in you.
And I am all
sunlight
and fire
and free.

{created by you // jayne}

When the rains do come,
I will hold onto you so tightly,
like tree roots intertwining,
keeping the mountainside
from falling away.

{stablilization // jayne}

People who say
love gives you wings
have never been in love.
I have not grown
any feathers,
though it would be
a simple feat.
I have no need for flying
because the sky
exists in me.
The sun is always rising,
making vapor of the dew.
And all that light and softness
comes from being in love
with you.

{no need for wings // jayne}

It took me years of running
before I learned how to
stop.
Where colors once blurred together,
I can now see
how each blade of grass
is its own shade of green
and bends in its own direction.

{the pace of nature // jayne}

In the night
the eyes cannot see
beyond the headlamps' beam.
But the heart knows
what's out there,
just past the edge of the road.
The heart hears
the leaves softly rubbing against each other.
It hears
the twigs cracking,
the moss springing,
the river rushing
and what puts its foot down to cross.
The heart vibrates
at the same frequency
as the crickets
and empties itself
beneath the cool glow of the distant stars.
It feels
the shimmering black stare
of the creatures who find peace in the quiet
and wait for the trembling car to pass and go.
The heart longs for the same.
The heart knows
what's out there,
just past the edge of the road.
The heart has never seen sunlight.
It was made to be home in the dark.

{nocturne // jayne}

There are those who seek
to emulate the snake,
which sheds its skin
in a matter of days.
But what lies underneath
is more of the same,
only it shines a little.
They leave old skins
in the past.
They call it a husk,
yet they never manage
to move on from it.
Their skin is the same,
only it shines a little.

I wish to grow
like a tree,
to keep the past
inside of me,
to let it strengthen me
as I stand taller
against the wind.
I care not for shining.
It always dims.
Let me be
a resilient thing.
Let people crane their necks
to behold me.
I wish not to shed
pieces of myself.
I wish to stay whole.

{new year, same you // jayne}

{Onyx & Amber}
@onyx_and_amber

Onyx & Amber, otherwise known as Tanya Wasyluk, is a writer and poet living in Boston, Massachusetts. The personas were created to represent the fragile yet ubiquitous duality of life—the balance between the darkness and the light. Onyx explores themes of wickedness, evil, addiction, mysticism, black magic, hopelessness and depression; whereas Amber explores themes of love, softness, feminism, sex, warmth and wonder. Her style plays with rhyme and meter, and often contains a riddle or dream-like quality. She works as a writer in advertising and is looking to publish her first novel soon.

it's the oldest story in the book
of evil vs. good,
two forces, rivals, waging war
in conflict misunderstood.

one is pure and filled with light,
though not white like most assume,
but a sienna soft, honey glow,
sacred as a mother's womb.

the other is cryptic,
witchcraft wicked,
temptation in the darkness of night.
spellbound by the moon, a chilling tune,
shadows that cloak the light.

and the two, they're beautiful,
onyx and amber —
dancing, battling to be free,
but one cannot live without the other
and both
are trapped
within me.

{chapter 1 // o & a}

i remember the summer of peach trees.
and lying under willows that wept,
making lanterns out of fireflies
in mason jars we kept.

mornings fragrant of fresh cut grass,
campfire smoke still in our hair,
i'd bury my nose in honeysuckle blooms
as we'd watch dandelions
float through the air.

we'd pick berries,
wild, right off the bush,
our fingers crimsoned stained.
and we'd laugh until our stomachs hurt
as we rolled in puddles after it rained.

the stars came out for us every night,
crickets would sing our lullaby,
just two girls who still believed
in sending wishes towards the sky.

and now it seems a lifetime ago
we'd hum along with buzzing bees,
whispering secrets, magic and mischief
in that summer of peach trees.

{summer of peach trees // a}

wicker baskets and queen anne's lace.
't a g   y o u ' r e   i t.'
bare feet chase.
moss-covered logs. babbling of the creek.
behind the kissing tree
boys & girls play hide and seek.

and the birds are always listening,
and the sun will bend its light—
stretch between the branches,
gold silk threading into night.

the ivy hides the poison.
the honey hides the sting.
and a million tiny stars dance along a single string.

whispers in the summer wind,
these nights will live upon your lips,
and dye as blackberry stains
fade upon your fingertips.

{blackberry days // o}

she wandered through the gardens
shimmering in the summer sun
botanical
       b o h e m i a
flowers opening one by one.

a kaleidoscope of colors,
climbing vines and bright fresh blooms,
lotus speckled lily pads
fragrant earth
and rose perfume.

and in pools of glimmering waters,
she swam carefree and in the nude,
buoying her heart with the
false promise of hope renewed.

then one day,
because of our neglect,
things were no longer as they seemed,
she surrendered to her imagination—

mother nature lost,
                in her favorite dream.

{paradise lost // o & a}

she was the velveteen rabbit.
unravelling at the seams.
and time was but a turning page
drifting through a dream.

she had chased the children
whose laughter glittered gold.
followed in their footprints,
ran too far into the cold.

and it happened quietly.
in a meadow stripped by snow.
fists unclenched and on her knees,
bone-raw and heartbeat slow.

velvet softness. wooden buttons.
fell to still, white earth.
one end and one beginning—
the year of my rebirth.

{becoming // o & a}

there was a little black bird
who sang her midnight tune
as we ran barefoot beneath the shadows
of the iridescent moon.

we twirled around the forest
and weaved between the trees
to meet the pretty-eyed boys
who would bring us to our knees.

drunk of whispers and cheap whiskey,
we were so excited we couldn't speak,
and he promised me the world
as he ran his finger down my cheek.

i could feel my heart trembling,
w e w e r e a w a k e !
            w e w e r e a l i v e !
and so our innocence slipped away
just as the morning sun arrived.

{night of the virgin // o & a}

we laid lazily in that meadow
in efflorescent june.
lulled to sleep by dragonflies
and wildflower sweet perfume.

the air was balmy,
summer haze,
sun dappled your face through trees,
a blue bird's song, serenade,
drifted silkily through the breeze.

i looked at you, eyes half-lid,
traced my fingers down your spine,
a languor love, drunk daydream,
burning for you to be mine.

you pressed your lips upon my skin,
tasted my salt and craved my spice,
we bloomed for each other for hours that noon
in dulcet paradise.

{the meadow song // a}

we exist in the spaces between stars.
for a breath. a blink.
the pauses that part words,
where we fall and how we sink and then we slip
into the void. suspended in mid-air—
sand in the hourglass
but we stay frozen there.
because time does not exist in the breaks within the clock—
the white within the seconds, where tick melts into tock.
the shift away from lavender as twilight tip toes home,
and dawn comes creeping in yet we still
find ourselves alone.
somewhere in the interlude,
we have carved a world that ours.

respite found in the stillness
of the spaces
b e t w e e n   s t a r s.

{aperture // o & a}

they sat together on a warm summer night
and watched the glittering trees.
chimes twinkled somewhere far away,
moved by a gentle breeze.

"i wish i could be a lightning bug,"
she said with a heavy sigh.

"why be the bug
when you can be the lightning,
and set fire to the sky?"

{the questions // a}

i still remember the secret path
that led to our old pine.
memories of august nights
when i was yours and you were mine.

your eyes, your lips, illuminated,
by the opal light of moon,
like the flower that only opens
in the fragile lux of noon.

that pine was where we grew roots,
the one witness to our affair.
we were a comet on the ground,
as brilliant and fleeting as we were rare.

and now strangers in the forest
will walk that path and never see,
the imprint in the grass beneath
what was always more
                    than just a tree.

{treehouse // a}

it was sea glass—
green and blue.
sex and saltwater,
the taste of you.

driftwood and feathers,
naked in bed,
hemp, silk and beaded,
weaved thread by thread.

and like seashells
i collected all the
promises you said.
and like cheap wine
i let it all
go straight
to my head.

{headrush // a}

i was desperate to drown in you.
and in the end,
all i would get
was an ocean of glass bottles
filled with promises
you would never keep.

{gulping // o}

i live deep within my dreams
surfing the fringes of my mind.
melting clocks and carousels
paradox of space and time.

my childhood home, with orchards lush.
ripe peaches, roses in bloom,
laughter echo while catching lightning bugs,
parents fighting in the other room.

faceless figures, those who i've loved,
those who i've lost and all before.
then crystal clear i see his face,
every eyelash, every pore.

how long have i been lost here?
quicksand sinking, sabotage—
how can we know for sure what is
a dream,
       a delusion,
                and a mirage?

{a surrealist's dream // o}

tell me where the thorns grow,
how the weeds wrap around your spine.
where has mold spread and found the heart
encircled by the vine?

breathe fire through the nettle
that branches through the lungs.
how can rib's cage protect
when the organs are being stung?

and skin unfurls like birch bark.
the womb a fallow field.
bones twig and blooms within the breast,
tree rings 'neath eyes, concealed.

black widow weaves her cobwebs
venomous silk within the veins,
and eats the cells one by one
until just carcass remains.

then winter's frost grows deeper,
crystallizing stem and soil, then root.
but the poppies provide the nectar, and the
d e e p   s l e e p ,
they call forbidden fruit.

{the cancer // o}

they say there is a potion
hidden deep within the trees.
a twisted, tangled forest that
will bring you to your knees.

dark desires and delusions,
deceptions you will find
unravel
      t h r e a d b y
                    t h r e a d
the inner workings of your mind.

can you brave the scream of silence?
isolation in the wild?
deafened by your heartbeat,
ego beckoned and beguiled.

but the potion is a ruse.
the true prize when you survive
is the lesson of the forest—
that we must suffer to feel alive.

{the silence & the scream // o}

render me breathless. suffocated.
tongue split in two.
moon coaxes mother ocean,
the current of you.
pull me like first light
draws me from a dream.
hook, thread and needle,
split open at the seam.

save me from the hollow
like ink to blank page.
silver pillars make rivers,
melt down the cage.
ravage the garden, the fields,
set fire to the wall,

if you're coming just to take,
you better take it all.

{devour me // o}

there is a shanty by the ocean
that used to be my home.
my favorite hideaway,
the smell of salt, sea glass and stone.

it hasn't always looked that way,
against the wind it once stood tall,
sunlight streamed through open windows
as the tides would rise and fall.

we'd spend lazy days
eating berries,
champagne drunk and making love,
and murmurings sweet nothings
under starlit skies above.

and although that time has come and gone,
and storms destroyed the land,
i'll still gaze upon that seaside shack
and see our castle in the sand.

{the broken-down place // a}

i live upon the breezes
of chimes twinkling far away.
i am a vagabond, a wanderer,
upon one path i'll never stay.

i am moss on abandoned train tracks
in the mountains, overgrown,
i am a midnight river
lined with graffiti-covered stone.

i am a bolt of lightning
that is gone before i start,
but i guess that's just the beauty
and the curse of a gypsy heart.

{not all who wander // o}

i am a work progress. a 'fixer-upper' type of home.
but i have a good foundation and a solid set bones.
weeds have grown around my spine, windows
s h a t t e r e d, like my heart. and you might find
decay if you rip my floors apart.
but there was once a time my roof was strong
and paint was bright. dust and cobwebs didn't swirl
within my lonely streams of light.
but no one sees that anymore,
they use me, then they leave.
but i could be a home again if someone would believe.

now i've locked my doors, i'm boarded up.
if you won't love me weathered and worn,
don't come as a stranger in the night
seeking relief
                  from the storm.

{w.i.p. // o}

i had spent a lifetime plucking petals.

he loves me,
       he loves me not.

until one day i realized
what a shame it was
to waste something so beautiful
on a question.

so i planted those flowers.
nurtured them.
and ever. so. slowly.
a love for myself
blossomed
in the glory
of the sun.

{self care // a}

i count my mistakes like stars.

but in the end,
they always fall in line
a n d c o n n e c t

to take the shape of
something beautiful.

{constellation // a}

let's bath ourselves in honey and steep rosehips
in our tea. add cinnamon for sweetness,
a cup for you, a cup for me.
words and words and words and words.
and a little ice cream, too.
we'll laugh until our stomachs hurt;
cry when those words are raw and true.

and we will dance and we will spill our wine,
the merlot showing on your cheeks.
the hair unshaved grown on our legs,
this is the best i've felt in weeks.
and m y g o d !
the time we waste on men!
sorting through who's bad, who's good,
perhaps the love we really need
is the strength of the sisterhood.

{fwb. // a}

we could learn a lesson from the willow
that starts as a fledgling tree.
sprouting from the soil
unsure of what it will come to be.

and with wisdom it grows taller,
as the weather folds its spine,
carrying on its shoulders
experience that only comes with time.

and it discovers in old age
a hard truth that's buried deep—
that despite the fleeting sunshine,
we are the most beautiful
when we weep.

{what the trees teach us // a}

let's have breakfast in the cosmos
you'll have coffee, i'll have tea,
we'll use stardust as our sugar
and sunbeams for honey.

instead of news, we'll read the stars,
a more credible source of fate—
and time will be a fallacy
erasing fears of running late.

we will marvel at our planet,
which at times feels dark and cold,
but from a distance we will realize
all the beauty that it holds.

and from this new point of view
we will feel how everything's connected—
funny the difference a morning can make
when you take a new perspective.

{panorama // a}

this is for the women
who are not afraid to roar.
who jump into the darkness
and believe that they will soar.

the wildflowers and wildfires, the
waves crashing into shore,
whose beauty and whose power
is impossible to ignore.

you are a woman and a wonder,
don't let them tell you otherwise.
you are
c e l e s t i a l,
you're a goddess,
a comet blazing through the sky.

so when you're in despair,
consumed by hopeless cries,
remember you are both
the might conqueror
and the prize.

{wildflowers & wildfires // o & a}

{Lauren Kaeli Baker}
@sweetbriar_june

Lauren Kaeli Baker lives in Australia but grew up in New Zealand, surrounded by green hills and the sea. She enjoys capturing moments and memories in both written and photographic form. Lauren has always found solace in nature and language, for their ability to put everything into perspective.

I know how to read the wisdom of rivers.
I know that their meandering,
their curved edges and bends are a sign
of old age.

I know that their murky silt-sodden depths
speak of lives well lived; the muddier the river
the more laugh lines.

I know these ancient rivers
have lessons for me:
I make notes of the way they run,
unhurried, slow and steady.

I highlight the margins of their meanders,
copying the faithful ways in which
they carve their own paths.

I am baptised by my local river
every morning when I shower and I let it
whisper its secrets into my skin.

{the wisdom of rivers // lauren kaeli baker}

I once learned from a broken woman
that gardeners know God differently.
With earthen crusted nailbeds
her green fingers planted seeds
in my mind.

I listened to her sermon and
I learned a thing or two.

In her religion, miracles
are the first green shoots,
grace is in the bloom,
faith is the courage by which
the flower holds its ground.

Worship is the breathing in
of sweet perfume
and the ability to grow
even when nobody's watching;
even when it seems
the odds are against it; even
when everybody is looking down
at the soil in doubt –
to grow anyway,
is nothing short of
divinity.

{what the broken woman taught me //
  lauren kaeli baker}

I marvel at the sun-sequinned sea
and smile when it waves; close my eyes
and let it rock me to and fro.
I'm sure that the shore is a magical place;
neither ocean nor land,
and lo,
here I stand: a foot in both worlds.

Salt-soaked serenity, I know
why ships are female.
When I listen to the ocean's song
building, rolling, breaking,
I swear I can hear She...
She,
She
is the salt and the buoyancy
and the wisdom and the abundance
and is maybe Mother Nature
in her favoured element.

There was a blind surfer on breakfast
television this week
and I thought,
how incredible to be one with this
magnificent body.
To divine its swells
and its unfathomable depth;
knowing it is treacherous
and still trusting it to carry you.

{she sells stories by the sea shore // lauren kaeli baker}

There is something so comforting about sunsets.
The reliable pattern of rise and rest,
regardless of the weight of the day.
Regardless of the weight on your shoulders.
The quiet grace by which it exits,
trailing a shawl of pink and drawing
the blue velvet curtains.
It's almost as if it's holding you
after a long day, which is to say, gently.
As though there'll always be tomorrow.

{hold me gently // lauren kaeli baker}

I mourned the loss of my marigolds.
Poured water on their empty graves.
Pulled out their dried mortal remains
and tossed them
without ceremony.

Every day I looked upon the space
where they once bloomed.
Moved the terracotta mausoleums
out of the sun.
Then into the sun.
And out again.

And when I finally accepted
that there was nothing I could do,
I devoted myself to nurturing
the other plants, who were patiently
awaiting my attention.

And then, a miracle.

The green shoot pushed through
that dormant bed
of soil and sphagnum moss.
Little by little it uncurled
towards the sun;
growing on its own,
opening with courage.
Blooming for no one
and no other reason
than the astonishing experience
of being alive in this world.
That is resilience.

And I make sure to cherish
these evanescent moments.
To celebrate my marigold.
To admire its colours.
To honour its independence
while still nourishing it with raindrops
collected in my watering can.
Because that is love

{the marigold// lauren kaeli baker}

It is early.
I have been up all night battling the darkness;
holding the light for the lost,
for the temporarily blind,
for the ones in the shadows,
for the ones who fear the shadows,
for the ones who are the shadows.

My light flickers
but I hold it steady.

The last few mornings have been drenched
in viscous fog, but today,
today the sun blooms before me,
a golden coin shimmering
just at the edge of the world
spilling peach juice across a canvas
of opalescent blue.

It stops me in my tracks
and I stand, weary, bleary,
reverent.
I almost feel I should drop
to my knees.
I want to run toward it,
grasp in my hands this astonishing light,
take it to my patients' bedsides
and pour it into a candleholder,
but I know I will never reach it,
so I make a sharp left
and walk up the hill, away
from the blossoming brilliance
of a new day.

For me, it is bedtime.

Now I am surprised to see the moon,
pearl lustre slung low
close by,
in a space of her own
in this blanket of sky.
From my humble place on earth
I can see the chickenpox scars
on her face – still beautiful.
She is over-polished,
part of her circle
wiped clean away – still whole.
I follow her up the hill
to my home.
Fortune favours me this morning.
My own light is replenished.

{sky poetry // lauren kaeli baker}

Re-potted some sage today,
willed it to sink its roots
into new soil.
Asked for some sage advice
on how exactly do to the same.
Waited for the storm as the wind
gusts blustered
as my skin shimmered under
the too hot sun and tendrils
stuck fast
to the back of my neck.

For all its fresh start metaphors
January feels a lot like questions
gaping for answers.
I remembered an old proverb
about winds of change,
walls and windmills, thought maybe
I need to embrace the uncertainty,
to let it happen since change
like the wind, can't be controlled.

I just need to spread my arms,
and cartwheel my way through.

{sage // lauren kaeli baker}

Where I come from in the upside
down, in the deep
deep south
of the planet
June is an ice queen.

She kisses you until
your lips turn blue, runs glacial
fingertips down your spine.
At night she holds you close
but in the morning you awaken
in an empty bed
still
shivering.
Listen
and you might hear
winter-bitten blades
of grass whispering her name.

She is the one who breathes
through the gap under your door,
numbing your toes,
chilling your bones.
She is hoar frosts
and verglas,
snowdrifts
and weeping windows.

June is the coldest of them all.
You must find your own warmth.

{june // lauren kaeli baker}

We'd sit side by side
gazing up at the night
and she'd tell me
that I was her brightest light

She'd wait patiently
for my eyes to adjust
and explain that we're made
from celestial dust

She assured me
that there was nothing to fear
because in the darkness
the stars are there

And if ever I was lost
or led astray
she'd tell me to follow
the milky way

She taught me
that if I closed my eyes
the moon would sing me
lullabies

And she'd say again and again
so forever I'd know
always look up, girl
you were made from that glow

{glow // lauren kaeli baker}

There is something sacred
about spring flowers.
The persistent ritual of deliberate bloom
on the back of a disintegrating winter.
The way in which we give them names
like T.S. Eliot named cats:
Magnolia
Jacaranda
Snowdrop and Tulip.
Do they have jellicle names? If only
all rebirths were as graceful.

There is something miraculous
about the way the universe unfolds,
how it gifts spring blossoms rain
and sunshine, then lets them grow
at their own pace. The ephemeral
lifespan; colourful confetti
decorating footpaths. If only
all endings could be so gentle.

{sacred spring // lauren kaeli baker}

The early evening falls quietly
and without fanfare.
It catches my eye by chance,
a shimmering shaft of golden light
on the wall by the stairs,
no more than thirty centimetres long;
the length and approximate width
of a ruler.

It dances against the wall,
cut by the shadow of the blinds,
silhouettes of trees
tremble together, dappling
the honeyed slip of sunlight,
branches bristling
with the first leaves of spring.

And before my eyes, the light fades.
It happens gradually,
and then all at once,
the way a season changes.
The way a building collapses.
The way a soul leaps
over the garden wall of a hospice
and disappears into the unknown,
leaving me staring
at the space it just occupied,
wishing I could've held onto it
a moment longer.

{the falling of light // lauren kaeli baker}

Fallen leaves,
thou art a heavenly reminder,
lying wretched and trampled on wet concrete
and gushing gutters that for all that lives
there comes an end.

And O, that which we grieve
is more the beauty with which thou wast
once strung in trees and less so
thy death itself,
which has been gradual and melancholy
and perhaps even a relief.

The pines shiver at thy passing;
there but for the grace of evergreen.
Lo, though thou art paper thin and lifeless
there is still beauty in thy fragile veins;
a lesson in acceptance and release

for all those who stop by
thine earthly mausoleum.
Perhaps this is why the most
inevitable verb
to leave
is named for thee.

{hymn for the fallen leaves // lauren kaeli baker}

Slowly
with meticulous attention
to the unfurling
and the hopeful
stretching toward the sun
resolute because no one
ever said it couldn't
colour spilling into stems
into stamens
into petals
reverence of raindrops
a christening of diamonds
sway briefly in the breeze
such beauty is short lived
soil
both cradle and grave

{how does your garden grow? // lauren kaeli baker}

Ask me where I worship and I'll tell you
about sunsets over water and the hymns of birds
and crickets. The baptism from a shower of rain and
the life cycle of deciduous leaves.

Ask me why I'm so sure God is love and I'll point to
the way the sun kisses the soil to make the plants grow;
the attentive symmetry of butterflies.

I'll remind you about photosynthesis, strong winds and the power
of gravity; wonders we can't see but know exist.

Ask me why I revere the universe and I'll explain
that the trees provide us with oxygen, that the moon pulls
the tides back and forth like a blanket and the stars
can be used as a compass.

Ask me about faith and I'll show you
how the baby bird flies for the first time.

Ask me my favourite psalm and I'll take you
to the water's edge, tell you to close your eyes
and listen.

{eden // lauren kaeli baker}

The last of the day star's stain bleeds out,
the once persimmon sky now a spillage
of blackberry juice.
The crickets sing outside
a chorus
of cheerful chirrups,
sharing their song
for no reason, aside,
from that the night is warm
and they are alive.

At the kitchen window
a praying mantis gives thanks
for the same thing.

{summer night in mt. wellington // lauren kaeli baker}

I could sit here
for hours,
with the sweet song of the sea,
watching the way it folds
onto the shore, as if making a bed
of golden sand and salt
laced lullabies

For hours
I could sit here,
flat plane of horizon
where ocean meets sky
and mermaids wish for human forms
the way we long for great depths;
that we may sea
beyond the surface

{solitude // lauren kaeli baker}

Followed the moon home tonight,
pearl brooch pinned to heaven's blouse.
Wandering through the city
in skipped-spring-altogether-summer heat,
past the bottle shop and under the bridge
broken fence posts and string light bars.
Friday the 13th bats squabbling among leaves,
shadows on the river, cloudless night.

I read that trees do their growing
by moonlight,
soaking up the atmosphere,
shrinking and
        e x p a n d i n g.
Hundreds of years old, some of them.
We all need the right environment to grow.

Keep walking.
        Breathe in.
Breathe out.

{friday 13th // lauren kaeli baker}

This morning the neighbour
took a knife to the trees,
hacking off rogue branches
broken in recent storms. He stood
atop the flimsy fence in bare feet,
holding a palm frond and bantering
with the man in the apartment above me;
a back lawn, two storeys and several years
between them.

I'd been waiting for the rain all day.

Now
I sit on the patio in the cool night,
staring at the space where he stood;
the ghostly glow of his television
visible between leaves and narrow trunks.
The trees drink raindrops
and rustle soft in the breeze.

I ask them,
Do you know the fate of your kind?
Can you hear them crying?
I ask them
Do you blame us?

The trees do not reply.
They give me oxygen all the same.

{asking the trees // lauren kaeli baker}

I read about the sugar maples in North America.
How they adapt to the shifting
of the seasons.
How they carpet the land in a blaze
of flaming metaphors.
Celebrated cycles – much more
than those of women and yet
still treated the same;
wounded with stakes
until they bleed syrup.
Beautiful on the outside;
useful for what they create.

There is more to a maple
than its inner sweetness, more to it
than its profound beauty.
At its core are stories.
Historical records of years lived,
of storms weathered.

I read that the sugar maples
are leaving New England
and moving west;
that climate change is forcing them
to put down roots in Oklahoma;
in Kansas.
I read that they're chasing the rain
and I sensed a kindred soul,
because I am too.

{moving maples // lauren kaeli baker}

The birches are shedding
and change is a light leaking
from the horizon.
Pioneer trees understand
growth and quiet determination,
dependable, placid despite their bark
which even dampened burns
so that you may see the future
by scrying in their flame.

Symbol of creation
of spirit
of strength

Some two hundred years ago
in the Highlands of Scotland
gentle Cameron hands abandoned
seeds upon hearing of royal landfall;
running headlong to an ill-fated war
of old versus new.

Still,
the birches grew.

{the birch trees that mark landfall //
lauren kaeli baker}

The rain never bothers knocking,
just arrives with hushed apprehension;
tears on windows
it puddles on the lawn around
the clothesline, seeps into the earth
draws out worms, calls down
the birds. Petrichor
perfume, heady and grounding
and lingering long after it's left.

It holds you while you cry
joyful tears
aching tears
and no one need know because
it always takes the blame

       the rain

never bothers to say goodbye
but always leaves a gift:
brilliant rainbow arches
crystalline silk webs
and flowers.

Always flowers.

{the rain // lauren kaeli baker}

He spills peach juice, the sun.
He spills peach juice on the surface of the water
and it shimmers.
It shimmers and the boats, they blush
pink and shy and the sea,
it carries them as though they have no burdens,
and I,
I sit in holy silence as the passage of time
unfolds before me.
And the others,
the lovers, the talkers,
the foodies and the long-time friends;
the gym bunnies and the dog walkers
and the dad racing his child on a pint-sized
scooter,
they don't notice.
Such is time.
The sun, he smears his peach jam hands
along the walls of the sky;
a toddler resisting bedtime,
and I wander.
I wander silently back to my motel,
where I sprawl on the king-sized bed,
feasting on cheap pink wine the colour
of a sunset,
and rapidly melting mint slices;
the chocolate equivalent of sand
slipping through an hourglass.

{the passage of time // lauren kaeli baker}

It is said that to see a leaf
falling from a tree means
a loved one is thinking about you
in the afterlife.
In this hallowed resting place
the trees are shedding;
a carpet of leaves underfoot,
where the dead are left in eternal
reminiscence.

I wonder who thinks of them,
these vibrant, complex human beings
who once had homes inside
living memories.
I run my fingers over names,
dates etched in stone and marvel
at how a lifetime can be reduced
to a short story.

I read their names aloud,
an incantation
of long forgotten appellations
and the leaves whisper them back to me.

The soil is a sanctum of tree roots
and old bones.

My friend once attended
the exhuming of a corpse.
She said the hands were still largely intact
and I thought - *of course.*
We are born grasping
and we die holding on.

{garden of bones // lauren kaeli baker}

Urban jungle,
ghost town of molten tarred roads
and empty swimming pools
peeling blue paint and traffic lights
controlling phantom cars, found
on the map just east of regret

Dead trees and parched patches formerly
rented by grass, concrete structures full
of desks no longer in use, keyboards
holding DNA and years old crumbs, plastic
waste skittering through barren streets

I once made a home in you,
found my own patch of green
by the river, near the sea.
I used to lie
on the ground, fill my eyes
with stars, fill my lungs,
my ears
my heart
with you

It's shameful,
truly

how we collectively watched
as you died.
Turned our backs and walked away.

Now there is not enough water
to absolve us.

{a letter to Brisbane in 2060
(if the estimates are correct) // lauren kaeli baker}

{Solace: Poetry of Nature // Baker}

In the end
oceans will swallow shorelines;
icebergs, the last few melting cubes
in a tumbler marked with human fingerprints

In the end
the trees will stop breathing
for us, and dried up grass will snap
like split ends on a brittle head of hair

In the end
the climate will be the thief of seasons
and animals will starve, entangled
in mankind's carelessness
strangled by plastic souvenirs
of consumerist culture

In the end
the people will be furiously planting
seeds in arid soil in a desperate bid
to save their home and messages
in plastic coke bottles from 1988
will all say it's too late

In the end
lullabies and poems will speak
of foreign things, like gentle streams
and blackbirds and lamb's fleece
white as snow

And the book will be closed
and sweet foreheads kissed
and in the dark, whispered words
the end

and there'll be no storytellers left
after that

{after the end // lauren kaeli baker}

{follow the authors}

To find more by these authors, please explore the following
social media accounts.

Kate Petrow	Instagram	@littlecloverleaf
		@kateloveskale_
Megan Patiry	Instagram	@meganrosepatiry
Amy Jack	Instagram	@embaark
Kait Quinn	Instagram	@kaitquinnpoetry
Elowen Grey	Instagram	@elowengreypoetry
Ashley Jane	Instagram	@breathwords
	Facebook	@breathwords
	Twitter	@breathwords
JaYne	Instagram	@_a.jayne_
Onyx & Amber	Instagram	@onyx_and_amber
Lauren Kaeli Baker	Instagram	@sweetbriar_june

Printed in Great Britain
by Amazon